While Grandma Is Sleeping

Written by Patricia R. Frank

Published by Orange Hat Publishing 2017
ISBN 978-1-943331-97-0

For information, please contact:
Orange Hat Publishing
www.orangehatpublishing.com

Orange Hat
PUBLISHING

www.orangehatpublishing.com

Katelyn, Lauren, Jimmy,
Lindsey, Natalie, Kelsey
My Dear Grandchildren,

All of you are Blessings from God, and I can't express how much I dearly love you, and I treasure the times we have shared together.

I know that the photograph was taken a long time ago, but I treasure it, too, because it was the one and only time we were all together.

One day, our Lord will call me 'Home' and I won't be able to talk with you in an earthly manner. But "While Grandma Is Sleeping" I pray you will remember me, and treasure my spiritual messages sprinkled with a little trivia and history.

As always, Love and God's Blessing!
Grandma Patricia

Table of Contents

I Will Lift Up My Eyes To The Hills

While driving home from church, I'm thinking about the beautiful message that I had just heard, and wondering how Lindsey and Lauren's proms went. While I was sleeping last night, granddaughters Lindsey and Lauren attended their high school proms. I pray they both enjoyed all the fun that a high school prom offers: dancing to their favorite music, having fun with friends, wearing pretty new dresses, and styling hairdos typically not adorned. But, most of all I pray that they and their friends all returned home safe and sound. I didn't just pray for Lindsey and Lauren, but also for granddaughter Katelyn who may have been out with her friends, or in her dorm, or possibly came home for the weekend to spend time with her mom. Grandson Jimmy was probably home with mom and dad, and granddaughters Natalie and Kelsey were probably home with mom and dad, too. Ah, yes, home safe and sound.

It doesn't seem that long ago when I, as a single mom, had three teens, and they were on dates or out with friends. Oh yes, those were some challenging years. I heard the back door open as each one came home. Being a very sound sleeper, you would think that I would sleep through our two big dogs coming down the stairs, prancing through the house, and greeting each one as they came in. But, like a baby's mother hearing that soft cry in the middle of the night, I knew when each one was home, and silently I would pray, "Thank You, Lord", "Thank you, Lord", and for the third time, "Thank you, Lord". And then they were all home safe and sound. A long time ago, but I remember it well.

It is even a longer time ago when I drove a country road to church. Actually, it was 48 years ago, and I have come to the realization that now I am 'on the right road'. Now I look at the hills and the countryside in a different way. Perhaps because I am older? No. Because I have grown wiser.

Those 48 years were my 'life enlightened' years, or you may call them my 'experiencing life' years. Now when I look at the countryside of hills covered with trees, I think of Psalm 121: "I will lift up my eyes to the hills; from whence cometh my help. My help cometh from the Lord, who made heaven and earth. He will not suffer thy foot to be moved; He that keepeth thee will not slumber. He that keepeth Israel will neither slumber nor sleep. The Lord is thy keeper; the Lord is thy shade upon thy right hand. The sun shall not smite thee by day or the moon by night. The Lord shall preserve thee from all evil; He shall preserve thy soul. The Lord shall preserve thy going out and thy coming in from this time forth, and even for evermore." Are my 48 years of 'life enlightened /experiences' noteworthy? Not at all! What is noteworthy, however, is that without the Lord's help, guidance, comfort, strength, protection, forgiveness, mercy, promises, and yes, some discipline, I would not be looking at these hills any differently now than I did 48 years ago.

My favorite verse in Psalm 121 is: "He shall preserve thy soul". What is the soul? Do we really have a soul? Yes, we have a soul! God put the first breath of life (the soul) into Adam, (Genesis 2:7), and man became a living being. And so, from the beginning with Adam, God has placed, and continues to breathe, the breath of life in each little embryo at the time of conception.

How does God preserve our souls? That is a very thought provoking question. God shares how precious our soul is to Him in Holy Scripture: Ezekiel 18:4 reads "Behold, all souls are Mine; -------The soul who sins will die". In Ecclesiastes 3:20–21 we read that when we die, our bodies shall return to dust. We often hear this at a gravesite committal ceremony: "From dust we came, and to dust we shall return."

But our breath (soul) will ascend to God, and our very soul will stay with God until He returns on Judgment Day. We read in Proverbs 24:12: "And does He not know everything, who keeps your soul." This truth is difficult for some to fathom, because mere man will no longer be 'in control' of anything, and that includes his soul.

We want to be such controlling people over our own lives, and over others, but when we die, God will be totally 'in control.' In 1 Peter 2:11, we hear, "Beloved, I urge you as aliens and strangers to abstain from fleshly lusts which wage war against the soul," and we are asked in Matthew 16:26, "For what will a man be profited, if he gains the whole world, and forfeits his soul? Or what will a man give in exchange for his soul?"

I thank God for my Christian heritage! Christian parents throughout time have set the stage for the Lord to preserve the souls of their children by bringing their infants to a baptismal fount.

Parents and Godparents speak for the infant, and through the Holy Spirit, the water, and placing the cross of Christ on that little forehead, the tiny infant has, through the rite of Holy Baptism, become a Child of God, and God has claimed him or her as His own.

As an infant grows, it is the responsibility of the parents and Godparents to help the child grow in the faith proclaimed and promised at baptism. We are born helpless, but with love and nourishment we grow in body, mind, and soul. Parents begin nourishing their children's souls by teaching prayers.

One of our first prayers is a beloved Evening Prayer. Let's pray it now, "Now I lay me down to sleep, I pray the Lord my soul to keep. If I should die before I wake, I pray the Lord my soul to take. Amen"

Ah, there is that word 'soul' again. There is a newer version of this prayer that doesn't make mention of the words soul or death. That is interesting but also disturbing. Did they eliminate those words because they do not want to explain them, or because they don't want to hear them?

The 'worldly' part of the very world that God created can't grasp its hands around the word 'soul' perhaps because they can't use it in some lucrative advertising ad as they do for other things that may enhance our mortal existence like with foods, drinks, diet plans, cosmetics, vitamins/supplements, exercise equipment, entertainment, or communication devices.

Some intelligent scientists can't develop a formula for the soul, and some mathematicians can't find a calculation for it; both sadly conclude that there is no existence of a soul because they cannot prove it with their wordly calculations.

The first life we live is the learning life - learning from our parents, some of our personality traits take form, and most certainly the education of our minds takes precedence; we are sent to school! Do parents ask their children if they want to go to school? I wasn't asked. Parents know when the time for reading, writing, and arithmetic has come, and off we go!

As young adults, we enter another stage of life, and now we learn that we need to care for our bodies. We nourish and take care of our bodies by maintaining proper diet and exercise, and in so doing we can enjoy a healthy and active lifestyle. We nourish our minds and look to higher education after high school to secure a great career. Or, we may pursue a vocation that doesn't require more education than a high school diploma. I fall in that category as I didn't like high school that much. There is, however, one thing that I regret about High School, and that took place when I was a junior. Writing a term paper was a requirement in junior English class, and I decided to write my paper on Walt Disney. I needed to go to the library to do research after school, which meant either my father or mother would have to drive into town to pick me up at the library. Attending High School in the 1950s meant the library was your only source for information as the Internet hadn't been invented yet. My English teacher was a very lovely, small-framed, dark-haired lady, had gorgeous clothes, and I believe she was probably Italian. I do remember her name, but prefer not to attempt a spelling of it. She gave me an A+ on my term paper, and I was honored when she asked if she could have it. Well, term paper time was over, I was dating, and next year I would be a senior; why not let her have it? That was then, but many times I do regret that I allowed her to keep it; I would have enjoyed reading it now and then to see why I deserved an A+ on it. Perhaps you may want to know, and perhaps you may not want to know, but I will share anyway: What made Walt Disney famous? Being very poor, looking for work as an artist, Walt Disney was sitting in an upper flat of a boarding house in St. Louis, and to his amazement, running across his drawing board was a mouse. Hence: *Mickey Mouse*

Let's continue where we left off after high school. Whichever avenue we travel, we want to work at a vocation that we enjoy, and one that will make us financially stable. It is admirable to set and achieve our goals, and our saving account has a glowing 'bottom line.' And all is well! But is it?

Have we given any thought to preserving and nourishing our soul? Are we getting bored with me addressing our 'soul'? In my "Reference Bible" there are more than fifty references for "soul," and there are less than twenty references for the word "body," and most of those pertain to the Lord's body, and not our earthly bodies. That lets us know how important our soul is to God.

Some individuals believe that once you die, you are dead, and others believe in reincarnation; neither is true! We read in Hebrews 9:27, "It is appointed unto man, once to die, and after that the judgment."

God tells us "that we are all sinful by nature", and in Psalm 51:5, "And in sin my mother conceived me: we daily sin much, and indeed deserve nothing but punishment, but thanks be to God who gives us the victory through our Lord Jesus Christ." St. Paul tells us in Romans 3:23, "For all have sinned, and fall short of the glory of God." And we read from 1 John 1:8, "If we say we have no sin, we are deceiving ourselves, and the truth is not in us." Because sin damages our soul, our sure defense is Jesus, and only through and with Jesus can our souls be nourished to withstand the world, the devil, and every temptation that comes our way.

And I can say in all honesty, and I quote 2 Timothy 3:15, "From a child I was taught the Holy Scriptures which are able to make me wise unto salvation." But Grandma still messed up, still does, we all do, and we always will! Without a nourished soul, my dear ones, brokenness of heart and spirit, trials and temptations, and shattered dreams can cause us feelings of despair, hopelessness, and devastation. With these come tears, anger, hatred, resentment, and revenge.

And, sometimes, we can be our worst enemy; Frank Sinatra sang it, "I Did It My Way."

Do we always want it our way? Maybe, just maybe, it isn't God's way. In Proverbs 16:9, we read, "The mind of man plans his way, but the Lord directs his steps." We should not feel at all surprised someday when we hear God gently whispering, "Oh, I wish you hadn't done that!"

God doesn't plan our consequences, but because of our actions there could be consequences on our horizon. Perhaps, though, consequences will be used by God to redirect our lives. We make our plans, and God doesn't need to check with us when He makes His plans. He tells us in Jeremiah 29: 11 "For I know the plans that I have for you, plans for welfare and not for calamity to give you a future and a hope."

Repentance! Tough word! Is repentance in order here? God will not forsake us, and will hear us when we ask for forgiveness. We find this comfort in Psalm 51:17: "The sacrifices of God are a broken spirit; A broken and a contrite heart, O God, Thou wilt not despise."

There may be people, even loved ones, who cause us despair, and hurtful feelings beyond our deserving it, and now we are left crying in the night. Or, our employer 'downsizes' the work force, and we lose our job. We can ask ourselves and God a million times, "Why did this happen to me? I didn't deserve this!" And with the tears we may feel anger, and perhaps, "I'll get even!"

We may plan a way to get even, and we may succeed, but is that what God would want us to do? Is 'getting even' God's way? Perhaps we are taking matters into our own hands, sadly, by trying to do it our way, which never seems to lead to a peaceful heart.

Our Loving God knows exactly what we are feeling, and how deeply we have been hurt. We listen to the Lord as He speaks to us to help us through our brokenness and sleepless nights.

Psalm 34:18 reads, "The Lord is near to the brokenhearted, and saves those that are crushed in spirit." The future may look very dismal, but we pray from Psalm 25:4, "Show me your ways O Lord; teach me Your paths."

Think about and visualize a colorful 'needlepoint' picture. Now only think about the back side of it. Stitching of all different colors of yarn, going in various directions, nothing makes any sense or has any design; it just looks like a mass of colored yarn. Many times we are looking up at the back side of such a mess, and visualizing it as our life, and saying, "My life is a mess." But not God! God is looking down at the beautiful front side of the needlepoint, and God is saying, "Everything is perfect; everything is in place."

Whatever we are experiencing, we trust God to lead us and help us through it. It could be feast or famine, and I've experienced both.

St. Paul tells us in Philippians 4:11-13, "Not that I speak from want; for I have learned to be content in whatever circumstances I am. I know how to get along with humble means, and I also know how to live in prosperity; in any and every circumstances I have learned the secret of being filled and going hungry, both of having abundance and suffering need. I can do all things through Him who strengthens me."

There is a beautiful hymn to soothe our souls, and let me share the first verse:

"When peace like a river attended my way;
When sorrows, like sea billows, roll;
Whatever my lot, thou hast taught me to say,
It is well, it is well with my soul."

God The Father The First Person Of The Holy Trinity

We were created by God our Heavenly Father to live forever! And, God created us for a purpose. It is not about us; it is all about God. We can believe that and accept it, or we can ignore it.

God does not care what job or career we have pursued, or whether we have acquired great wealth or are as poor as a church mouse. This life here on earth prepares us for our eternal life. Focusing on God during our life will indeed prepare us for eternity with Him.

In Psalm 16: 8-9 the psalmist tells us what he has done, and we pray to do the same, "I have set the Lord continually before me; because He is at my right hand, I will not be shaken. Therefore my heart is glad, and my soul rejoices; my flesh also will dwell securely."

I need to share a favorite verse from Jeremiah 29:11 again. God tells us, "For I know the plans that I have for you, plans for welfare and not for calamity to give you a future and a hope." God looks into our hearts and minds, and tells us exactly that in Psalm 139 when he says, "He searches us and He knows us. He knows when we sit down, and He knows when we lay down. Before a word is from our tongue, He knows what we will say. Such knowledge is too wonderful for us to understand. We can't flee from His presence. God knows our inward parts, because He wove us in our mother's womb, and our frame was known by Him when we were made in secret. We should be thankful that we are so wonderfully made, and our soul knows it very well. God has written in His book the number of days ordained for us. The thoughts of God are so precious; they are too many to count, and they would outnumber the sand. God will take a stand against the wicked and men of bloodshed among us."

The last two verses are a beautiful prayer. Verses 23-24 read, "Search me, O God, and know my heart; Try me and know my anxious thoughts; And see if there be any hurtful way in me, and lead me in the everlasting way." I do encourage you to read the Psalm in its entirety.

In Proverbs 19:21 we hear, "Many are the plans in a man's heart, but the counsel of the Lord, it will stand." Yes, we make our plans, and yet sometimes God needs to alter those plans if He feels they are not for our best eternal interest. There is a beautiful Prayer of Serenity; I do not know who wrote it, but it brings me a lot of comfort. "God grant me the serenity to accept the things that I cannot change. courage to change the things I can change, and the wisdom to know the difference."

This is where choices and consequences come into play. We may make some bad choices, and then find consequences that are difficult to deal with. Yes, God knows we will 'trip and fall,' but relying on God to help us through difficult consequences will strengthen our faith and our relationship with Him.

Of course, consequences could be more serious than just getting a speeding ticket; we tell ourselves we won't speed again, but we still have to pay the cost of the citation.

God not only created us, but sometimes His direction in our lives molds us to an increased and more resilient faith in Him. In Isaiah 64:4 we find words that remind us of God's direction in our lives: "But now, O Lord, Thou art our Father, we are the clay, and Thou art our potter; And all of us are the work of Thy hand." In Romans

8:28 St. Paul assures us, "And we know that God causes all things to work together for good to those who love God; to those who are called according to His purpose."

Think and consider why the first three of the Ten Commandments which God wrote pertained to Himself. God made us in His image; did He not have the Divine Right to command us to obey Him?

The First Commandment: "Thou shalt have no other Gods before Me." Was He just referring to the golden calf that the Israelites had built? No, He was already referring to other structures that would represent a god to some people. And He was already referring to some modern day gods; our time could be a god; not taking time for Him, our job, our money our recreation, and anything else that we put before Him. God is commanding us to fear, love, and trust in Him above all things.

The Second Commandment: "Thou shalt not take the name of the Lord thy God in vain." When we say "Thank God it's Friday" is it a prayer or are we looking forward to our weekend? And perhaps we won't say "God" during the weekend unless we are angered about something.

I heard my father and mother express anger, but they never used the Lord's name in vain. My mother would merely say, "That would make a minister curse." My father used three German phrases, and as I grew, and started to understand the German language, I was able to translate them into English. None of those phrases contained any cursing or swearing either. Allow me to translate the three phrases for you. 1) For discipline: "I can't believe you did that; you know better!" 2) Working on farm machinery: "Why did that have to happen now!" And, 3) When you wanted to go somewhere that he didn't feel comfortable with or if you wanted to buy something, he made your decision for you: "You are not going there; that's no place for you." And "You don't need that; you are not spending money on that."

God is further commanding us in the Second Commandment not to practice superstition, lie, or deceive by using His name. We should only use His name in every trouble, pray, praise, and giving thanks.

The Third Commandment: "Remember The Sabbath Day to keep it holy." God wants us to worship Him. Not to despise His Word, but to hold His Word sacred, and gladly hear and learn it.

The remaining seven commandments pertain to honor, obedience, and love for and toward all people.

There are two questions that God will ask us on Judgment Day, and He has already told us what those two questions will be.

The first one: "What did you do with My Son Jesus Christ?"

The second one: "What did you do with the life I gave you?"

God reveals those answers in 2 Thessalonians 1:8-9 and in Ecclesiastes 3:17.

2 Thessalonians 1:8-9 reads, "Dealing out retribution to those who do not know God, and to those who do not obey the gospel of our Lord Jesus. And these will pay the penalty of eternal destruction, away from the presence of the Lord, and from the glory of His power."

And, again, verse 12 reads, "In order that the name of our Lord Jesus may be glorified in you, and you in Him, according to the grace of our God and the Lord Jesus Christ."

Ecclesiastes 3:17 reads, "God will judge both the righteous man and the wicked man, for a time of every matter and for every deed is there." God already knows about the deeds that we have done, and the life we have lived, but He will ask us to declare and give an account of them anyway.

God's love for mankind was written about throughout the entire Old Testament by the Prophets. God's love, again, was proclaimed throughout the New Testament in the glorious birth, life, death, and resurrection of His Own Son Jesus Christ, in the teachings of Jesus, and the preaching by the apostles.

In Ecclesiastes 1 we read that "God has set eternity in our hearts, and God wants us to rejoice and do good in one's lifetime." And "I have seen that nothing is better than that man should be happy in his activities, for that is his lot."

When we have the joy of the Lord in our lives, our lives will be more meaningful and fulfilling, and we won't wake up someday and ask, "What on earth am I here for?" or "Why am I doing the same old same old every day?"

There was a song out a few years ago, and it had a much depressed message; one phrase particularly that was heard was "Is that all there is?" For some people life may be just that: 'this is all there is'. If only they knew, and let us never forget that the life God gave us is a precious gift from Him, and the way we live our life, and the way we become is truly our gift to God.

Then, and only then, will the joy of the Lord be our strength, enable us to walk humbly before God, and enlighten us to be imitators of Jesus' life and teachings. These will give purpose and meaning to any career, any activity that we enjoy, any hobby/sport, and most importantly to raising a family.

Whatever we have, whatever we do, and how we do it should always bring glory to God!

Always remember that God sent His Son Jesus, and Jesus said, "I have come that they may have life; and that they may it more abundantly."

Jesus didn't just mean here on earth, but He meant that we have an 'abundant eternal life'.

That is 'Where' God meant for us to live forever!

Jesus The Son Of God
The Second Person of
The Holy Trinity

Anyone can, and many do, and some are already, encouraging others only to refer to Jesus as a teacher, a good and law abiding person, and a friend to many people while He lived on earth. What a pitiful description of our Jesus!

Throughout the entire New Testament Jesus personifies that He is the Light of the World, He is the Living Water, He is the Bread of Life, He is the Truth, He is the Way, He is the Good Shepherd, He is the Lamb of God, and He is the Resurrection and the Life.

There has been some controversy in the news as to what ethic color Jesus was.

If you have ever been in a Sunday school room with preschoolers, you will soon discover that Jesus can be any color that is available in a box of Crayons. If some ethnic children see Jesus as the same color as their skin, Jesus won't mind; He only wants all nationalities to come to know Him. And, as the song goes, "Black or yellow, red or white; all are precious in His sight."

Should that controversy ever arise in a discussion, and someone may want an opinion; we merely need to remind them that Jesus was a Jew. It is okay if you don't want to share Jesus' genealogy, but Jesus' genealogy can be traced back to

King David, and the account can be found in Matthew 1:1-17. Holy Scripture does not offer too much information about Jesus' earthly father, Joseph, but we know from Biblical history that Joseph was of the house and family of David. At the same time as Jesus' birth a decree was issued by Caesar Augustus that everyone needed to go to their own city or lineage to be registered. Therefore, Joseph had to go to Bethlehem, and Joseph took Mary with him to whom he was engaged, and the account of Jesus' birth from Luke Chapter 2 tells us that Mary was with child. Therefore, the prophecy from the Old Testament in Micah would be fulfilled; The Messiah would be born in Bethlehem.

Jesus is sometimes referred to as 'a carpenter's son', leading us to believe that Jesus' earthly father, Joseph, was a carpenter. There is a comical scene in the movie "The Passion" starring Mel Gibson between Jesus and his mother Mary. Jesus shows His mother a chair that He made in his father's carpenter shop. Mary finds the whole idea of a chair amusing, because in all of Judea in those days there wasn't anything that resembled a chair; people reclined and sat on the floor. Jesus only grinned at her with a quizzical look as if to indicate that perhaps someday there could be such a thing as a 'chair.' It is a heartwarming scene between Jesus and His mother.

After Jesus arose from the dead, and before His Ascension, He appeared to His disciples. I find this account so inspirational and want to share it from John 20:19-29: "When, therefore, it was evening, on that day, the first day of the week, (it must have been Easter evening), and when the doors were shut where the disciples were for fear of the Jews." Let us imagine being in that room with the disciples!

The disciples had very good reasons to be afraid! The two soldiers guarding the tomb had undoubtedly told the Roman and Jewish leaders that the tomb was empty, and perhaps they were already receiving severe punishment for not guarding the tomb properly. Perhaps the Roman leaders thought that the eleven disciples had rolled away the stone, and had sent soldiers out looking for them. The disciples knew that they had not rolled the stone away from the tomb, and the Jewish leaders didn't believe Jesus when He said that the 'temple' would be destroyed, and that in three days it would be rebuilt; Jesus, however, was referring to His body as the 'temple' and not the temple for worship in Jerusalem, but the Jewish leaders didn't understand what Jesus was referring to.

Peter had seen the empty tomb, and, of course, Mary had told the disciples that she had seen the Lord. And being very fearful, the disciples must have been discussing and asking themselves, "So, if He isn't in the tomb, where is He?" They had heard Jesus preach, had seen His miracles, had followed, had trusted, had become so devoted to Him, had believed so deeply in Him, and then they saw their Lord arrested, tried, and brutally killed. Then suddenly, Jesus appeared, was standing in their midst, and said, "Peace be with you." Jesus showed them His hands and His side, and we read the disciples rejoiced upon seeing the Lord.

Thomas was not with them, and when the disciples told Thomas that they had seen the Lord, Thomas told them that unless he would see Jesus for himself, he would not believe. The account says that it was eight days later, and this time Thomas was with the disciples. Jesus appeared again and said, "Peace be with you" Then Jesus said to Thomas, "Reach here your finger, and see My hands; and reach here your hand, put it into My side; and be not unbelieving, but believing." Thomas answered, "My Lord and MY God." In John 20: 29 Jesus tells Thomas, "Because you have seen Me, you have believed. " The last sentence of this verse is for us! "Blessed are they who did not see, and yet have believed."

Sometimes we sit alone and are afraid because of situations, problems, or concerns that we are currently experiencing. Then we need to sit quietly, and listen for the voice of Jesus, "Peace be with you, I know what is on your mind, and what is concerning you; I am here."

And, how much does our Jesus love us? He would say, "See" as His arms are stretched out with hands nailed to each side of that cross, "This is how much I love you!" We all need to remember, when life causes us to fall flat on our faces, those Everlasting Arms will pick us up, help us stand, and hug us while we are sobbing.

The following account from St. Paul's letter to the Philippians is very explicit as to who Jesus really was, still is, and will be forever. Philippians 2:8-11 reads, "And being found in appearance as a man, He humbled Himself by becoming obedient to the point of death, even death on the cross. Therefore also God highly exalted Him and bestowed on Him the name which is above every name, that at the name of Jesus every knee should bow, of those in heaven, and on earth, and under the earth, and that every tongue should confess that Jesus Christ is Lord to the glory of God."

There is a beautiful message in a hymn written by a gospel group.

"There's Something About That Name"
"Jesus, Jesus, Jesus! There's just something about that Name!
Master, Savior, Jesus! Like the fragrance after the rain.
Jesus, Jesus, Jesus! Let all heaven and earth proclaim!
Kings and kingdoms will all pass away, But there's something about that Name!"

The Holy Spirit The Third Person of The Holy Trinity

Pentecost was God's almighty power of the pouring out of The Holy Spirit.

The account from Acts 2 tells us that devout men from numerous nations had come to Jerusalem, and while they were gathered, there suddenly came from heaven a violent rushing wind, and it filled the whole house where they were. And there appeared to them tongues as of fire distributing themselves, and they rested on each one of them. The multitude was bewildered, because they were able to understand each apostle speak in their own languages.

Peter, addressing the assembly, proclaimed the Gospel of Jesus Christ, and we read that many were baptized, praised God, and continued to devote themselves to the apostles' teaching and fellowship, to the breaking of bread and prayer. And the Lord was adding to their number day by day those who were saved.

Why isn't Pentecost, this outpouring of The Holy Spirit, as popular as Christmas or Easter?

There isn't any benefit in celebrating Pentecost because the secular world can't promote clever advertising for attractive decorations and gift giving which will generate record sales for retailers.

Only the church holds Pentecost very sacred, because the church regards The Holy Spirit as the one Significant Force that sanctifies, empowers, enlightens, and increases faith in the hearts and minds of those who seek to stay steadfast to the Gospel of Jesus Christ.

Had it not been for the Holy Spirit, men of God would not have written The Law of the Old Testament or The Gospels of the New Testament.

The Holy Spirit has enlightened men and women through the ages to speak out, to preach, to write about, and to guide believers and bring non-believing young and old individuals to the saving grace of our Lord Jesus Christ through Baptism and into the Christian Faith.

We are inspired by The Holy Spirit when we pray in reverence for someone or something in Jesus' name, and we know that our petitions will be heard by God Himself. Can we truly grasp such a beautiful realization?

What keeps our dear Christian missionaries in war-torn countries? I can't even fathom their faith, and them knowing that they may be persecuted and even killed for their faith.

Our missionaries must be saying as St. Paul wrote in Philippians 1:21-24, "For me to live is Christ, and to die is gain. But if I am to live on in the flesh, this will mean fruitful labor for me; and I do not know which to choose. But I am hard pressed from both directions, having the desire to depart and be with Christ, for that is much better; yet to remain on in the flesh is more necessary for your sake".

St. Paul was imprisoned, beaten, and persecuted for preaching Jesus' saving Gospel, and he knew if he would die he would be with Christ, but if he would live he could continue to preach.

I believe that these encouraging verses from St. Paul and The Holy Spirit keep our missionaries persevering in their faith to offer comfort and support with prayers to fellow Christians amidst the horrors of war. One day Jesus will be saying to our dear missionaries, too, "Well done good and faithful servants; come enter the kingdom prepared for you!"

It is The Holy Spirit waking one up on a Sunday morning without an alarm clock. It is, also, the work of the Holy Spirit working in your mother when she calls, "It is time to get up to go to church." (Now you know you can't blame your mother anymore).

When I was growing up, there were no options; my wonderful Christian parents were totally inspired by The Holy Spirit to keep The Sabbath Day holy.

I remember, too, that one of the parishioners from our church would be at church an hour before worship services to ring the church bell. The ringing of the bell invited the community to attend our worship service which would begin in an hour. Perhaps the ringing of the church bell caused some residents in the community to be inspired by The Holy Spirit to attend worship services.

We no longer hear the ringing of any bells as in the past. Could it be that the residents in communities are now disturbed by the fact that the bells are waking them earlier on a Sunday morning than they wish?

The Holy Spirit is represented as a white dove, and in the "Spirit Song" it is brought to mind. "Oh, let the Son of God enfold you with His Spirit and His love, let Him fill your heart and satisfy your soul. Oh, let Him have the things that hold you, and His Spirit like a dove, will descend upon your life, and make you whole."

Let's pray the last verse of another beautiful hymn, "Come, Holy Spirit, aid us to keep the vows we make; this very day invade us, and every bondage break. Come, give our lives direction, the gift we covet most; to share the Resurrection, that leads to Pentecost."

May we take to heart what St. Paul tells us in Romans 5:5, which reads, "God's love has been poured into our hearts through the Holy Spirit which has been given to us," and in Galatians 5:22 we find the fruits of the Holy Spirit which are love, joy, peace, patience, kindness, goodness, faithfulness, gentleness, and self-control. If we live by the Spirit, we will walk by the Spirit.

Let's never underestimate the power of The Holy Spirit; It could be that The Holy Spirit may be the One who encourages us to open the doors of our hearts when we hear Jesus knocking.

I know, full well, that it was The Holy Spirit who encouraged and inspired me to write these 'messages', and I sincerely pray that all I have written will glorify God.

All of you know how much Grandma enjoys taking pictures; maybe I will take a little credit for adding the pictures.

The Sun, The Moon, and The Stars

Once, while on a cruise ship, I saw the sun in its magnificence arise over the Caribbean. When I saw the sky light up over that huge body of water, I could only think of one thing - the beautiful hymn, "My God How Great Thou Art." Another time I saw the sun set off the island of Maui, and again the words came to me upon seeing the awesome picture God had painted over the Pacific.

How can anyone dispute, deny, or not believe in God when just thinking about the sun. The sun arises each and every morning without fail since God said, "Let there be light!" God allows the sun to rise on those who believe in Him, and on those who do not believe in Him. God does not withhold the dawning of a new day from anyone. The God who many believe does not exist created the sun that can illuminate the earth as the sun orbits around it. Mere man, with his highest degree of knowledge or intelligence, couldn't even imagine inventing a light with such powerful illumination.

And again, each evening the brilliance of God's miraculous creation appears in the sky as we see the beauty and mystery of the moon and stars. I am again reminded of another phrase of the hymn: "I see the stars, I hear the rolling thunder, Thy power throughout the universe displayed." Man can build spaceships, but God in His infinite wisdom created the sparkling stars. We read in Psalm 147:4, "He counts the number of stars; He gives names to all of them." And in Psalm 19: 1, "The heavens declare the glory of God, and the firmament showeth His handiwork."

Then one day, and Jesus is very clear about this in Matthew 24:29-30 when He speaks about His glorious return, "...THE SUN WILL BE DARKENED, AND THE MOON WILL NOT GIVE ITS LIGHT, AND THE STARS WILL FALL from the sky, and the powers of the heavens will be shaken and then the sign of the Son of Man will appear in the sky, and the tribes of the earth will mourn, and they will see the SON OF MAN COMING ON THE CLOUDS OF THE SKY with power and great glory."

We read in 2 Peter 3:10, "But the day of the Lord will come like a thief, in which the heavens will pass away with a roar and the elements will be destroyed with intense heat, and the earth and its works will be burned up."

I do get annoyed with the people who get 'bent out of shape' regarding global warming, and I would just like to share with those individuals sometime that when the earth burns up, (and not to make fun of it), but that will be global warming at its finest and final hour.

Perhaps one day all people around the world will come to realize in Whose world they are living, and we sing it,

"This is My Father's world; oh let us not forget,
though the wrong seems oft so strong, God is the Ruler yet.
This is my Father's world; why should my heart be sad?
The Lord is King, let heaven ring; God reigns, let earth be glad."

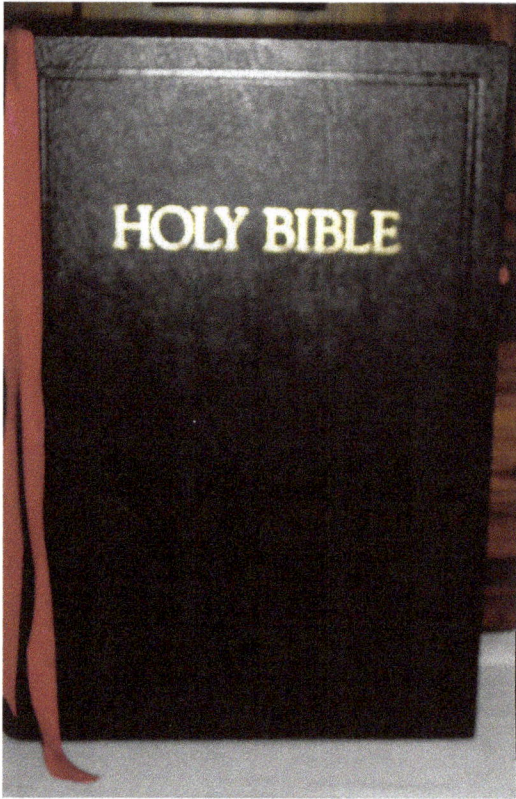

The Holy Scriptures/The Bible

Who wrote the Bible? The Bible tells us.

2 Peter 1: "For no prophecy was ever made by an act of human will, but men moved by the Holy Spirit spoke from God."

And who were these men who were inspired by the Holy Spirit?

First there were the prophets of the Old Testament that had actually talked with God, walked with God, some who were defiant to God, and still others who were disciplined by God (which was the case of Jonah).

Also, in the Old Testament you will find 'the God inspired wisdom' which was written by King Solomon in Proverbs and Ecclesiastes.

King Solomon only asked God for wisdom, and indeed these two books express God given inspirational wisdom.

The New Testament was written by the apostles of Jesus. And, if we really think about it, why wouldn't the apostles have written everything down that they had seen, heard, and witnessed while being in the very presence of Jesus.

What an unbelievable blessing that must have been for them.

Sometime between 1517 and 1520, a German monk at Wartburg Castle in Germany first translated the New Testament from Greek into German, and later translated the Old Testament from Hebrew to German.

With the invention of the printing press, the Bible was translated from German to

English. The Bible is now written in 1,300 languages. The Bible has been threatened many times, and it has prevailed, and continues to stay in existence. Stalin, in Russia, had the Bibles burned. Hitler just totally outlawed them, but neither leader succeeded in destroying God's word.

God commands that the authority of Scripture stands. The very last book of The Bible states it very clearly; Revelations 22:18–19 reads, "I testify to everyone who hears the words of the prophecy of this book; if anyone adds to them, God shall add to him the plagues which are written in this book. And if anyone takes away from the words of this book of prophecy, God shall take away his part from the tree of life and from the holy city, which are written in this book." This command from Revelations should make it very clear, and yet many do not understand that not one word can be added, and that nothing can be taken from it.

It is troubling how some want to condone social issues that are contrary to God's word. The lifestyles and choices some people make is between them and God. Their argument is with God if they cannot accept the authority of scripture as it was written. And then, what is even more troubling is that those who take a stand against social issues that are contrary to God's word are considered judgmental against the people who make choices. Jesus warns us about judging people, and throwing stones, just as He did in telling the people who were about to stone a woman for adultery. Jesus said, "He who is without sin, cast the first stone at her!"

It is sad to say, but the Bible is under attack right here in America today! We hear that some are suggesting that the Bible is merely a 'book of opinions,' and this is very disturbing. Webster's Dictionary defines an opinion as 1. personal belief, 2. personal evaluation. Does this mean that we can believe and adhere to whatever suits us? When someone offers an opinion in a conversation, we can believe it or not; after all, it is only their opinion. I wonder how God feels about this new wave of thinking that the Bible is only someone's opinion, or are we telling God, "I will abide by this one law, but this other one can't apply to me because 'this' is now 'socially and politically' correct."

St. Peter refers to the living and abiding word of God in 1 Peter 1:24-25: "For all flesh is like grass, and all its glory Like the flower of grass. The grass withers, and the flower falls off, But the word of the Lord abides forever". In Hebrews 5: 12-13 St. Paul speaks about the Bible having special power: "For the word of God is living and active and sharper than any two-edged sword, as piercing as far as the division of soul and spirit, of both joints and marrow, and able to judge the thoughts and intentions of the heart. And there is no creature hidden from His sight, but all things are open and laid bare to the eyes of Him with whom we have to do."

God gave us our minds and reasoning abilities; anyone who wants to dispute the Living Word of God has that option.

We are also hearing about an organization that is now opposing the availability of Gideon Bibles in hotel rooms, wishing them removed because they are offensive. For eleven years I frequently stayed at hotels, and I would on occasion read from the Bible in the room. So why have these Bibles become offensive? Is it because these individuals don't want to read them, and they don't want others to be encouraged to read them? Or, is it that they don't want to be reminded that there just could be a God? I have seen many drawers in hotel rooms; if the presence of the Bible is so offensive, why not just open a drawer, and slide it in! I do not know how many hotel chains will succumb to removing the Bibles from their rooms, but it is aggravating.

Beware, my dear ones, as to how far organized groups will go to destroy our Bibles, and not just in hotels. Treasure your Bibles; read them often, use sticky notes to refer back to favorite readings, and if the pages get tattered, God won't care.

Why is it that more people do not read the Bible? People read to be informed whether it be for news events, or to become more knowledgeable of things that concern them, or to stimulate and improve their intelligence, and to be entertained.

All are great reasons! But, why not read the Bible?

One may be surprised how interesting, and yes, even entertaining, some of the accounts are regarding the people who lived in the Old and New Testament times.

One beautiful story in the Old Testament is the book of Ruth. How about a quick 'book report?'

A husband, his wife, and two sons left Bethlehem because of a famine in Judah. In the land of Moab both sons married Moabite women. The husband and both sons died, and the wife Naomi was returning to Bethlehem. Naomi urged both of her daughters-in-law to remain in Moab; one remained, but Ruth, loving her mother-in-law pleads to go with her, telling her," Where you go, I will go, where you lodge, I will lodge, your people shall be my people, and your God shall be my God." In Bethlehem, Ruth began working in the fields owned by Boaz, a wealthy landowner. Boaz and Ruth married, and had a son Obed. Obed had a son Jesse, and Jesse, of course, was the father of King David making Ruth King David's great grandmother. The book of Ruth is four short chapters; I still enjoy reading it! Just a note; the words spoken by Ruth are often used in marriage ceremonies.

Reading and studying the Holy Word of God allows the wisdom of God, which surpasses all human understanding, to keep our hearts and minds focused and centered on our Lord and Savior Jesus Christ in all we do, in all we say, and in our very being.

There is a great deal of difference between intelligence and wisdom; intelligence is many times so intent and concerned about its own being and achievements that it gets in the way of true wisdom and can't grasp the understanding of wisdom. The wisdom of God surpasses intelligence.

I heard something a long time ago, and have never forgotten it. I heard that when Ernest Hemmingway, author of numerous novels, was lying on his deathbed, he asked for 'the book.' Those at his bedside asked, "Which book?" thinking he was referring to one of the novels he had written. Hemmingway replied, "There is only one book; the Bible." Perhaps Ernest Hemmingway had done as Jesus instructs us, also, in John 5:39: "Search the Scriptures, for in them you will have eternal life, and they are they which testify of Me."

And so my dear ones, if your Bibles ever come under attack, and I pray that that will never happen, you will have the words written on your hearts.

Worship The Lord In The Beauty Of Holiness
Remember The Sabbath Day To Keep It Holy

Psalm 121:1 reads," I was glad when they said, let us go to The House of The Lord." Psalm 100: "Shout joyfully to the Lord, all the earth. Serve the Lord with gladness. Come before Him with joyful singing. Know that the Lord Himself is God; It is He that has made us, and not we ourselves. We are His people and the sheep of His pasture. Enter His gates with thanksgiving, and His courts with praise. Give thanks to Him; bless His name. For the Lord is good; His loving

31

kindness is everlasting, and His faithfulness to all generations."

To worship The Lord in His Majesty is not only a privilege and a joy, but God commands it of us in the Third Commandment. How hard is it to keep the Sabbath Day holy when Sunday is the only day of the week that we can sleep in? We need to get up early weekdays for school or work, and Saturdays may have its priorities. Do I understand that thinking? Not buying into either of those.

This is a good time to share some family genealogy.

In 1846 a family fled from Germany, and one of their children was their six year old son (my great grandfather). Along with them were numerous other families from Germany and other countries throughout Europe. This particular family loved their native Germany, but like many European people, they were becoming more and more subjected to political and religious oppression.

They had an opportunity to flee to America, and it meant a long voyage by ship across the Atlantic Ocean. They arrived in New York, and persevered westward to Wisconsin where they could again work as farmers as they had done in Germany.

The six year old son grew into manhood, got married, and purchased a farm in the same community. The Lord blessed him and his wife with eleven children... Good thing the farm house had seven bedrooms!

FYI: Cows need to be milked every morning and every evening, and I am certain you understand that this includes Sundays. After the Sunday morning milking the family would attend worship services.

Of these eleven children, six were boys. As the six sons grew, they could help their father expedite the milking on Sunday mornings.

My grandfather was one of those six sons, and as he got older, he remained on the family farm to continue farming.

He got married; he and his wife had six children. The family tradition continued.

After Sunday morning milking, the family attended Worship Services.

Only one of these six children was a boy (my father), and he remained on the family farm to continue farming. He married, and he and my mother had a mere three children, of which I am the oldest.

Again the Sunday morning tradition continued; after milking we attended worship services.

Why this genealogy? Religious Freedom!

Let's go back to 1846. Arrival in America for my great great grandparents meant that God had not only protected them on their long voyage, but He had indeed blessed them that they could again work as farmers, raise their families, and above all there would no longer be any threat to their Christian faith. How could they not, each and every Sunday, worship God with thanksgiving and praise, and teach their children to do the same?

Do we take worshiping God for granted? Do we say, "I can go next Sunday"? We may have good intentions, but, when does next Sunday come? Maybe in a month or longer? We know what it tells us in Matthew 26:41: "The spirit is willing, but the flesh is weak."

We can't allow ourselves to get into the habit of staying away from church and not worshiping God. And as habits go, it will be easier and easier to stay away from attending worship services.

It is disturbing to see how slowly, but surely, we can see some political and religious opposition taking place here in our dear America. There has even been some talk during news broadcasts that IRS agents may be visiting churches in order to find out if what clergymen are preaching is 'politically correct.' Really?

What happened to separation of church and state?

There is an article in our constitution demanding that the government not interfere with religious freedom. What are the intentions of such an extreme move? Of course, such an extreme move should be brought before Congress. But will it? If a president wants to sidestep Congress, he only needs to write an executive order, and such a move could become law, and on the following Sunday, IRS agents could be walking into churches with notepads. Should an IRS agent visit my church he or she will hear the Gospel of Jesus Christ preached in its truth and purity.

We read in Luke 15:7, "I tell you that there will be more joy in heaven over one sinner who repents, than over ninety-nine righteous persons who need no repentance."

There would indeed be reason for rejoicing if upon hearing some clergy's message, an IRS agent returned to where he or she is living to seek out a church to attend.

Let's remember that the Apostle Matthew was a tax collector.

Will a day actually come when a church can be held liable for speaking out against something that is now considered politically correct, but is contrary to God's Holy Word?

Some even say that we are living in a 'post Christian era,' and if this is the case, it could be, in comparison, like a "Creeping Jenny" in our lawn which can choke out all of the grass. This is what could have happened in Europe, except many people fled to America. But what if this happens in America? Where will future generations of Christians flee to? There is no place left on the planet to go!

I will not know your grandchildren or their grandchildren, but they will all be a part of me. Or should I just not be concerned about their salvation, because I won't know them anyway?

Or, I could say, "It is your responsibility, because they are your children." Both of those statements would be self-centered, self-serving, and selfish of me only to be concerned for two or three generations.

My great great grandfather and my great grandfather never knew me, and neither were only concerned about their generations! I know because I knew my grandfather and my father weren't just concerned about their immediate generations either.

Now, here I am, 'an oldtimer,' and very concerned about future generations? Yes, I am very concerned.

I pray as I read in Ephesians 3:15, "To Him be the glory in the church and in Christ Jesus to all generations forever and ever." And in Philippians 2:15, "That you may prove yourselves to be blameless and innocent children of God above reproach in the midst of a crooked and perverse generation among whom you appear as lights in the world."

I, also, pray that you, your children, and all future generations may be such 'lights' in their generations.

We know we live in this perverse generation when we see huge billboards this 2014 Christmas season that say:

"All I want for Christmas is to skip church. I no longer believe in fairy tales"

There is something ironic about the wording though; they didn't omit CHRIST (as one might think they would) from Christmas, and I am thinking this was done on purpose to let people know that they believe that Jesus' Holy Birth is a fairy tale. This is a 'terrible sign' of things to come!

We need to pray for these individuals, and hope that one day they could take part in the beautiful Christmas season starting with Advent, and the lighting of an Advent candle each Sunday leading up to Christmas, hear some Christmas concerts, see a children's program as they share Jesus' birth as only children can, attend a Candlelight Service on Christmas Eve singing "Silent Night," and then feel the jubilance of a Christmas Day worship service. That is truly celebrating the rebirth of our Lord and Savior Jesus Christ.

That is Christmas! No fairy tale here!

All the beautiful hymns we sing at Christmas are so much a part of our Christian heritage, but there is one that celebrates not just our faith, but our forefathers' faith, and I pray that it will be sung for generations to come. "Faith Of Our Fathers" "Faith of our fathers! We will love; Both friend and foe in all our strife; Proclaim Thee too, as love knows how; By saving word and faithful life. Faith of our fathers, holy faith; We will be true to Thee till death."

I have attended worship services with a joyful heart, I have attended worship services with tear-filled eyes, and I am not exempt from having attended worship services with anger in my heart.

Psalm 84 offers all of the answers we need for the longing to worship whether we come with a joyful heart or a broken heart; Psalm 84:1-2 reads, "How lovely are the Thy dwelling places, Oh Lord of hosts! My soul longed and even yearned for the courts of the Lord; my heart and my flesh sing for joy to the living God." And again in Psalm 84:10-12, "For a day in thy courts is better than a thousand outside. I would rather stand at the threshold of the house of my God, than dwell in the tents of wickedness. For the Lord God is a sun and shield; The Lord gives grace and glory; No good thing does He withhold from those who walk uprightly. O Lord of hosts, How blessed is the man who trusts in Thee!"

Our favorite football team can win or lose on any given Sunday, but by attending worship we will always have a 'winning' Sunday!

Perhaps the message, or a hymn, or a prayer will touch our hearts, and soothe our souls, and upon leaving a worship service we feel inspired and encouraged to meet a new week with its joys and challenges, and undoubtedly there will always be some.

You will find yourself walking closer to God, even though God has been there all along.

We close this message with a song in our hearts:
"Just a closer walk with thee, Hand in hand we'll ever be;
Daily walking close to Thee. Let it be, Dear Lord, let it be.
In Thy care I want to be; Grant it Lord, this is my plea.
Give me light that I may see; As I walk, dear Lord close to Thee."

The 12 Disciples/Apostles of Jesus

We don't know too much about the prior lives of some of the disciples before Jesus called for them to follow Him. We don't know why Jesus chose twelve, and it was never mentioned in the Bible. Perhaps it had something to do with there being Twelve Tribes of Israel from the Old Testament.

The disciples were as follows: Simon (whom Jesus gave the name of Peter), James and John (the sons of Zebedee), Andrew (brother of Peter), Philip, Bartholomew, Matthew, Thomas, James (the son of Alphaeus), Thaddaeus, Simon (the Zealot), and Judas Iscariot.

We know that Peter, Andrew, James, and John were fishermen, and when Jesus found them by the seaside and told them to follow Him, they laid down their nets and followed Him. Jesus told them they would be fishers of men. The only other disciple we know about is Matthew, and that he was a tax collector.

Peter was probably the most colorful, outspoken, daring, and ready to take matters into his own hands. Peter, when seeing Jesus walking on the water toward the boat, was the one who conjured up enough faith to ask Jesus if he could get out of boat to come to meet Him, and Jesus said, "Come."

While Peter kept his eye on Jesus he was actually walking on the water, but when a wave came up, Peter, taking his eyes off Jesus, lost faith, and he began to sink. Jesus reached out His hand, and helped Peter back in the boat. A lesson here to remind us that when we take our eyes off of Jesus, our faith becomes weak, and we can sink into a life of hopelessness.

Jesus, on one occasion, asked the disciples, "Whom do people say that I am?", and the disciples told Him that people thought He was a prophet. Then Jesus asked the disciples whom they thought He was. Peter was the first to respond, "You are the Christ, the Son of the Living God!" Jesus told Peter that he would be the 'rock' on which He would build His church.

Peter was the one who drew a sword and cut off a soldier's ear during Jesus' arrest in the Garden of Gethsemane. Peter was the only disciple named who went to Jesus' trail. Peter, who once said "Lord, I will never deny you!", failed miserably by denying Jesus three times during Jesus' trial.

Jesus looked at Peter, and then Peter remembered that earlier Jesus had warned him about doing just that. We read that Peter went out and wept bitterly. Peter who endured beatings and had faced death at Herod's hand still continued to proclaim the Gospel of Jesus.

The Bible doesn't say, but history has it recorded that Peter was crucified, but he requested to be crucified (not like Jesus), upside down.

There is a novel entitled "The Big Fisherman" relating to Peter. Some, of course, is fiction, but there are many religious events in the novel as well.

The Apostle John was the only one named who stood at the foot of the cross at Jesus' crucifixion with Jesus' mother, Mary. The Gospels of John, 1 John, 2 John, were written by the Apostle John, and it is believed that the Apostle John also wrote the book of Revelations.

The early church believed that the Apostle John was banished to the Isle of Patmos.

The last scene in the movie "The Son Of God" brings tears to one's eyes as we see an aging and frail John sitting on this desolate island with only rock formations behind him, and as he is looking out over the large body of water surrounding the place, he sees Jesus appearing on the water. As Jesus is walking onto the sand and toward him, John's face beams with an exuberante joy that words can't explain. John sees and knows that his Lord and Savior is coming to take him 'Home', and his exile is finally over. You can almost hear Jesus saying to John, "Come, enter the Kingdom prepared for you."

Did Judas not know that his Lord would have forgiven him for betraying Him for 30 pieces of silver? Judas had heard Jesus preach and had seen the miracles which Jesus performed, but we read after the soldiers arrested Jesus, "Satan entered Judas' heart, and he went out and hanged himself." What a pitiful ending to a disciple who had walked with Jesus.

After Jesus' ascension, the disciples felt that they were in need of a disciple to replace Judas, and they actually found two worthy candidates. One was Barsabbas, and the other one was Matthias, and the disciples decided to cast lots for them. They prayed to Jesus before they cast lots, "Thou Lord, who knowest the hearts of all men, show which one of these two Thou hast chosen."

I suppose the disciples felt that Jesus would be in control of the lot falling to the man that Jesus would select if He were still with them.

Acts 1:26 tells us, "And they drew lots for them, and the lot fell to Matthias, and he was numbered with the eleven apostles." An interesting thing though; there is not another mention of Matthias after this, making it quite evident that Matthias wasn't whom Jesus wanted to replace Judas.

Jesus knew exactly whom He would choose to replace Judas, and Jesus found a man named Saul on a dusty road to Damascus. Was Saul an unknown or a commoner like the other disciples? Not at all! Saul was a very prominent man, known throughout Judea, Jerusalem, and that region for hating the followers of Jesus, and all those who were preaching and baptizing in the name of Jesus Christ.

Saul was feared and ruthless, not only for hating the followers of Jesus, but also because he persecuted them, and authorized to have them put to death without any remorse. Saul was held in high regard by the Romans for his persecution efforts. Saul was present, and praised by witnesses at the stoning death of Stephen, who was a young preacher and devoted follower of Jesus.

In Acts 9:1-19 is the account of 'The Conversion of Saul' on the road to Damascus.

Jesus calls to Saul, "Saul, Saul, why are you persecuting Me?"

Saul in freight falls to the ground becomes blind, and asks, "Who are you?" Jesus answers,

"I am Jesus of Nazareth, whom you are persecuting."

It is an emotional account, and I urge you to read it for yourself.

Saul became St. Paul who became the greatest of all the apostles. In 1 Timothy 1:15-16 St. Paul confesses,

"It is a trustworthy statement, deserving full acceptance that Christ Jesus came into the world to save sinners, among whom I am foremost of all. And yet for this reason I found mercy in order that in me as the foremost, Jesus Christ might demonstrate His perfect patience as an example for those who would believe in

Him for eternal life."

It is interesting to note that the above verse is written in St. Paul's letter to Timothy. Timothy was a young preacher of the gospel of Jesus Christ, and St. Paul urges and keeps encouraging young Timothy to continue in his preaching. Sometimes we may wonder how many times St. Paul recalled another young follower and preacher of the gospel of Jesus Christ, namely Stephen, whom he (then Saul) had authorized to be stoned to death. Perhaps that is why St. Paul is referring to himself as the foremost of all in verse 15.

A most inspiring hymn of confession and repentance is "Chief of Sinners, Though I Be", and continues, "Jesus shed His blood for me."

Truly a hymn written for the life, the conversion, and the faith of Jesus' greatest apostle - St. Paul.

A hymn that we, too, can relate to when confessing our sins, being repentant, and seeking forgiveness.

Most of the New Testament is comprised up of St. Paul's Letters. In St. Paul's letter to the Ephesians is the beautiful message which our Christian faith is based on. Ephesians 2: 8-9 reads, For by grace you have been saved through faith; and that not of yourselves, it is the gift of God. Not as a result of works, that no one should boast."

St. Paul was arrested many times, beaten, imprisoned, and finally put to death for the sake of preaching the gospel of "The Lord who had found him on that dusty road to Damascus."

I think about the Apostles when I sing the song, "Here I Am Lord." Jesus had commanded and commissioned the apostles to go into all the world and preach His Holy Gospel to all people. The first verse of this song is the Lord speaking, "I, the Lord of sea and sky, I have heard My people cry. All who dwell in dark and sin, My hand will save. I, who made the stars of night, I will make their darkness bright.

Who will bear My light to them? Whom shall I send?"

The response from the apostles is the Refrain: "Here I am Lord, it is I, Lord. I have heard You calling in the night. I will go, Lord, if You lead me. I will hold Your people in my heart."

Christian missionaries have responded, too, and have persevered dangerous regions and people, because of the inspiration of the Holy Spirit, and Jesus' words in Matthew 9: 37-38 "The harvest is plentiful, but the workers are few. Therefore beseech the Lord of the harvest to send out workers into His harvest."

And in Matthew 28:19-20, Jesus commands, "Go therefore and make disciples of all nations, baptizing in the name of the Father, and the Son, and the Holy Spirit, teaching them to observe all that I commanded you; and lo, I am with you always, even to the end of the age."

Is the Lord, perhaps speaking to us, too? Is He asking us to bear His light in our lives? Are we responding? "Here I am Lord, I will go Lord, if You lead me. I will hold Your people in my heart."

The Lord's Supper

In the night in which He was betrayed, Jesus gathered with the twelve disciples in an upper room and instituted The Lord's Supper.

We read in Luke 22:19-20, "And when He had taken some bread and given thanks, He broke it, and gave it to them saying, 'This is My body which is given for you; do this in remembrance of Me.'" And in the same way He took the cup after they had eaten and said, "This cup which is poured out for you is the new covenant in My blood for the forgiveness of sins; do this in remembrance of me."

When we come to The Lord's Table seeking forgiveness with a penitent heart, and we truly believe that Jesus' body and blood are present in the bread and wine, we receive full forgiveness and are sanctified with God's grace.

This is when we truly believe as God spoke in Isaiah 1:18, "Though your sins are as scarlet, they be as white as snow; Though they be red as crimson, they will be like wool."

Jesus welcomes sinners, all sinners, to His table, and He says, "Come!" Only Jesus can look into the hearts, the minds, and the souls of those approaching His Table, and there is no need to mention just the individuals listed in 1 Corinthians 6:9-11, but let's add ourselves to that list, because we are all inclusive and in need of God's forgiveness through Jesus' Holy Body and Blood, and no one should be denied. It is the Lord's Supper; not a church's supper, not a congregation's supper, but The Lord's Supper.

All of the disciples, including Judas, were seated at the table with Jesus. Did Jesus deny Judas the bread or the wine knowing full well that Judas would betray Him in the Garden of Gethsemane later that evening? Perhaps Jesus offered Judas an opportunity for repentance!

No human can look into the heart of a stranger, a guest, visiting a church seeking repentance, thus denying him or her Jesus' body and blood.

In Hebrews 13:1-2 we are encouraged, "Let love of the brethren continue. Do not neglect to show hospitality to strangers, for by this some have entertained angels without knowing it. "

Let us remember, again, that the Heavenly Angels will rejoice over one lost soul seeking forgiveness.

What A Friend We Have In Jesus

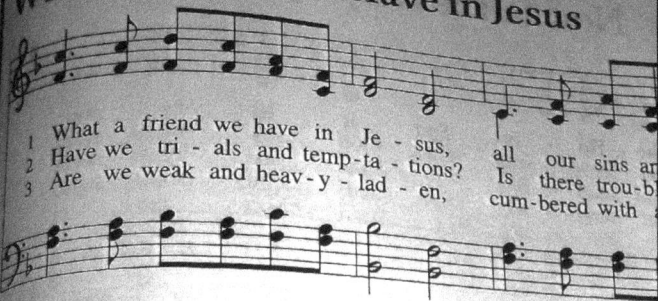

What a Friend We Have in Jesus

1 What a friend we have in Je - sus, all our sins and...
2 Have we tri - als and temp-ta - tions? Is there trou-b...
3 Are we weak and heav - y - lad - en, cum-bered with...

What a priv - i - lege to car - ry ev - 'ry-thing...
We should nev - er be dis - cour - aged— take it to...
Pre - cious Sav - ior, still our ref - uge— take it to...

Oh, what peace we of - ten for - feit; oh, what nee...
Can we find a friend so faith - ful who will al...

Webster defines a friend as: 1. a person who likes or is helpful to one. 2. a supporter or sympathizer.

Some people have kept friends since childhood. Some people make lasting friendships while going to high school, college, or in the workplace. In a deep-rooted friendship there is love and trust for each other. Sharing each other's happiness and sorrows can strengthen the friendship. Mistrust, hurt feelings, and sometimes even new friends of one or the other can threaten an existing friendship. We treasure our friends, and we want them to treasure us, too. When a friendship does dissolve, we experience sadness, an emptiness, and, yes, even anger and disappointment, especially if we were not responsible for the broken friendship.

Making new friends is sometimes fun and stimulating, but can we share and talk to new friends with the same trust and confidence that we did with longer known friends?

My grandma Ruth once shared a poem with me: "Remember always and bear in mind, a faithful friend is hard to find; so if you find one good and true, forget not the old one for the new." I do not know who wrote the poem. Grandma Ruth just said from memory.

Jesus is our One True Friend, and we can always trust in sharing our joys, our sorrows, our broken hearts, and our anger with Him.

Don't we sometimes feel better and relieved when we have truly 'vented' our inner thoughts and concerns regarding issues to an 'earthly friend'? Then, why not 'vent' those same inner thoughts and concerns with Jesus? What makes us think that Jesus doesn't know what is going on in our lives? Jesus rides in the car with us! Is that a bit frightening? He listens to our phone conversations, He knows what we will be texting even before we text, and He listens to our music! OH MY! Jesus sees what we are watching on TV and what games we are playing on the Internet.

I think I am counting correctly in saying that I have had eleven cars to date, and in all of them I have had conversations with Jesus. I have shared many joyful events, prayers of 'thanks,' a lot of tear-filled moments, and I have shared my anger, too.

In Isaiah 41:10 God says "Do not fear, for I am with you." And in Psalm 56:8, "You have taken account of my wanderings; put my tears in Your bottle."

Oh, how much we wish problems would go away quickly, but they do not! I remember a clergyman saying once, that we should give your problems, concerns, and anxieties ten minutes, and then give them to God in fervent prayer.

Tell God, "I just can't deal with this, please help me!" God assures us in 1 Peter 5: 6-7, "Humble yourselves, therefore, under the mighty hand of God, that He may exalt you at the proper time, casting all your anxiety upon Him, because He cares for you."

We sing an encouraging hymn: "What a Friend we have in Jesus, all our sins and grieves to bear. What a privilege to carry everything to God in prayer. Oh, what peace we often forfeit; Oh what needless pain we bear, all because we do not carry everything to God in prayer."

Jesus Knocking At The Door

Have we truly invited Jesus to enter our hearts and our lives?

We see Jesus standing at the outside of a door. The door represents the door to our hearts. Jesus is gently knocking waiting for an invitation to enter.

We can't see from the picture, but there is no handle on the outside of the door.

Jesus can't open it from the outside, and Jesus won't force His way in. The door of heart can only be opened from the inside to welcome Jesus.

Jesus doesn't care how old the heart may be or what color of skin the person has; Jesus only wants the heart to open the door, and receive Him as his or her Lord and Savior.

What is going on behind that door that Jesus' knock can't be heard?

Is our heart feeling such emotional hurt, and has depression taken over our minds that perhaps we are throwing a pity party celebrating 'woe is me'?

Another reason we may not hear Jesus knocking is because we are so angry, and we are so busy doing some 'construction' work. "Construction work? "Perhaps we are building 'dams'; beavers are great wildlife engineers in building dams for their purposes, and waterway dams are constructed by human engineers. We can be engineers, too, in building 'dams.'

'Dams' to hold up anger, animosity, hurt, bitterness, and even plotting revenge. When we open the door of our heart to Jesus and allow Him into our hearts and lives, He can help and show us how to build 'bridges,' enabling us to forgive, to find renewed hope, and peace of mind, and then we can, with Jesus beside us, walk over those 'troubled waters' that we were so desperately wanting to 'dam' up. An unforgiving heart could suffer eternal damnation.

Perhaps we are really troubled over our past, and we can't forgive ourselves. That is best reason of all to 'open that door', and pray from Psalm 25:6-7, "Remember O Lord Thy compassion and Thy loving kindness. For they have been from old. Do not remember the sins of my youth, or my transgressions; according to Thy loving kindness remember Thou me." And we can hear Jesus say, "Call upon Me in the day of trouble, and I shall deliver thee, and thou shalt glorify Me."

Nothing is too hard for the Lord to help us through when we allow Him into our hearts and lives. Wouldn't we open the door of our home to our mother or father, or a close friend to share our frustrations and hurt feelings with them? Why then, when we hear Jesus' tender knock, would we not open 'the door of our hearts' to Him?

Or, perhaps we are totally 'in control' of our lives, and things are going just great, and, yes, we know about Jesus, but right now we do not want to be bothered with getting to know Him any better than we already do. We believe in Jesus, and that is enough.

Listen very carefully. Are you sure He isn't out there knocking?

Jesus, The Good Shepherd

John 10:14 "I am the good shepherd; and I know My own, and My own know Me."

John 10:27-28 reads, "My sheep hear My voice, and I know them, and they follow Me; And I give eternal life to them, and they shall never perish; and no one shall take them out of My hand."

John 10: 11 reads, "I am the Good Shepherd, and the Good Shepherd lays down His life for the sheep."

Throughout the Bible, there is a great deal pertaining to sheep and shepherds.

Why shepherds? Shepherds were regarded with low esteem, and being a shepherd certainly was not a prominent position to hold.

King David was a mere shepherd boy, and the account from 1 Samuel tells us that God sent the prophet Samuel to Bethlehem to a man named Jesse to find and anoint the next king for Israel from among Jesse' sons. Jesse had seven of his sons pass before Samuel, but all seven were rejected (not by Samuel, but by God). Samuel asked Jesse, "Are these all the children?" Jesse told Samuel, "there is another in the fields tending the sheep, and Samuel had Jesse send for David who appeared ruddy. The Lord said. "Arise, anoint him, for this is he." And so, the ruddy shepherd boy became King over Israel.

King David encountered many problems; adultery and murder were two that he created for himself. The Prophet Nathan was sent by God to confront King David and expose his many sinful deeds, and disobedience to God's Law. David being a gifted musician is probably why his musical talent and sincere repentance led David to write many beautiful Psalms; actually, 53 of the 150 Psalms were written by David. Psalm 23, which the picture illustrates of The Good Shepherd, is by far the most often spoken; I invite you to read the psalm slowly, thinking about each verse, what the verses reflect, and what the picture illustrates as David is expressing it, "The Lord is my shepherd, I shall not want. He makes me to lie down in green pastures; He leads me beside quiet waters, He restores my soul.

He guides me in the paths of righteousness for His name sake. Even though I walk through the valley of the shadow of death, I fear no evil; for Thou art with me; Thy rod and Thy staff, they comfort me. Thou prepares a table before me in the presence of my enemies; Thou anointed my head with oil; My cup overflows. Surely goodness and loving kindness will follow me all the days of my life, And I will dwell in the House of the Lord forever."

As we look very closely at that lamb in Jesus' arm, this could be the lamb that went astray, and the one that Jesus refers to when He says in Luke 15:4-7, "What man among you, if he has a hundred sheep and has lost one of them, does not leave the ninety-nine in the open pasture, and go after the one which is lost, until he finds it? And when he has found it, he lays it on his shoulders, rejoicing. And when he comes home, he calls together his friends and his neighbors, saying to them 'Rejoice with me, for I have found my sheep which was lost.' I tell you that in the same way, there will be more joy in heaven over one sinner who repents, than over the ninety-nine righteous persons who need no repentance." God wanted King David back in His 'fold,' thereby sending Nathan as a 'good shepherd'.

We learn about lowly shepherds on the hillside outside of Bethlehem tending their flocks by night, and the heavens burst open with Heavenly Angels announcing,

"For unto you is born this day, in the City of David a Savior Which is Christ The Lord!" These lowly shepherds were the first to hear of Jesus' birth, and we read that the shepherds ran with haste!! Hymns and songs at Christmas tell us about shepherds; some of my favorites include: "While Shepherds Watch Their Flocks By Night", "Rise Up Shepherd", "Go Tell It On The Mountain" and "The Little Drummer Boy".

I remember a touching phrase from a Christmas song that was sung by a choir I belonged to, and the story tells us about a poor shepherd boy who had come to the stable, and he felt humiliation and worthlessness when seeing the beautiful gifts of gold, frankincense, and myrrh that the Three Wise Men had brought to Baby Jesus. The poor shepherd boy had no gift for Baby Jesus, but the beautiful ending is that the poor shepherd boy gave Baby Jesus his heart. When we first started rehearsing that song, I became very emotional, because the story was so moving. Let's just think about how many 'hearts' our Risen Good Shepherd would welcome, not just at Christmas, but throughout each year.

Are there 'good shepherds' among us today who need to look for lost sheep in order to bring them back into the 'fold'? Yes, a clergy who notices that a church member no longer worships, and possibly a parent can be a shepherd wanting their son or daughter back in the 'fold', because a child has gone astray.

Do we know Jesus as our Good Shepherd, and do we portray a 'Good Shepherdly Image' in how we conduct ourselves in our caring and courtesy of others, and through our word choices? Is it 'cool' to follow and share Jesus in our current high tech society? If we share an iPod song, a latest movie that we saw, or a new purchase we made at the mall with a friend, why not share Jesus? We may never know how much one of our friends may need our Good Shepherd if we don't share Him.

There is a beautiful hymn which is really a prayer with music.

"Savior, Like A Shepherd Lead Us, much we need Your tender care. In Your pleasant pastures feed us, for our use Your fold prepare. We are Yours; in love befriend us, be the guardian of our way; keep Your flock, from sin defend us, seek us when we go astray. You have promised to receive us, poor and sinful though we be; You have mercy to relieve us, grace to cleanse, and power to free. Early let us seek Your favor, early let us do Your will; Blessed Lord and only Savior, with Your love, our spirits fill."

Looking at that lamb in Jesus' arms, again, brings to mind that lambs and sheep were sacrificed through burnt offerings for praising and thanking God throughout the Old Testament. God provided a Ram in the thicket for Abraham when Abraham was about to offer up his son Isaac to God. Abraham named that place, and as it is still said today, "The Lord will provide." When we are in need, we know that somehow God will provide in His own way, and His Good and Gracious Will will be done in our lives. In Exodus we read about God's will being done in order to free the children of Israel from slavery in Egypt. Moses being sent by God had pleaded with Pharaoh numerous times, "Let my people go!" Pharaoh would not listen to Moses, and so God had a 'plan';

God always has a 'plan!'

In Exodus 12 we read about The Passover which is still a Holy and Religious Holiday for the Jewish people. God instructed Moses and Aaron to tell the children of Israel to kill an unblemished lamb, and to put some of the lamb's blood on two doorposts and lintel of their homes in which they would eat the lamb. God's judgment would pass over the land of Egypt, and the lamb's blood was a sign that God would pass over their homes, and the plague that would come upon Egypt would not harm the Children of Israel. And so it happened that God did pass over Egypt, and God struck down the first-born in the land, both man and beasts, and against all the gods of Egypt.

And so God carried out His judgment. Can we even comprehend God's anger, and how He deals with disobedience? Did the children of Israel fear God? They did, as we still do, but fear is removed when we obey God. The children of Israel obeyed God, and did what Moses and Aaron had instructed them to do. Pharaoh didn't fear God; Pharaoh thought himself as a god, but God proved Pharaoh wrong.

King Solomon wrote about fear in Proverbs 9:10: "The fear of the Lord is the beginning of wisdom, and knowledge of the Holy One is understanding." One of the most inspirational teachers I have ever had was at our parochial school, and he would many times quote Proverbs 9:10. Of course, when one is only in 7th and 8th grade, one probably fears a teacher more that God at that point in life. But it is an interesting verse, and it expresses not just a fear of God for obedience, but also for living. We should obey our parents or we could sustain some punishment. We need to obey the laws of our country, thereby staying law abiding citizens, or we could sustain even more serious punishment. Through obedience we need not fear God, our parents, our teachers, nor the men and women in law enforcement.

Even though we hold the Old Testament times and prophecies sacred, sheep and lambs are no longer sacrificed, because God provided the last Sacrificial Unblemished Lamb, and that was Jesus. God, in Jesus, sacrificed Himself and carried all our fears, and our sins to the cross in our place, and on the Easter we celebrate The Lamb of God - Jesus' Glorious Resurrection.

And I pray as in 1 Peter 5:4, "And when the Chief Shepherd appears, you will receive the unfading crown of glory."

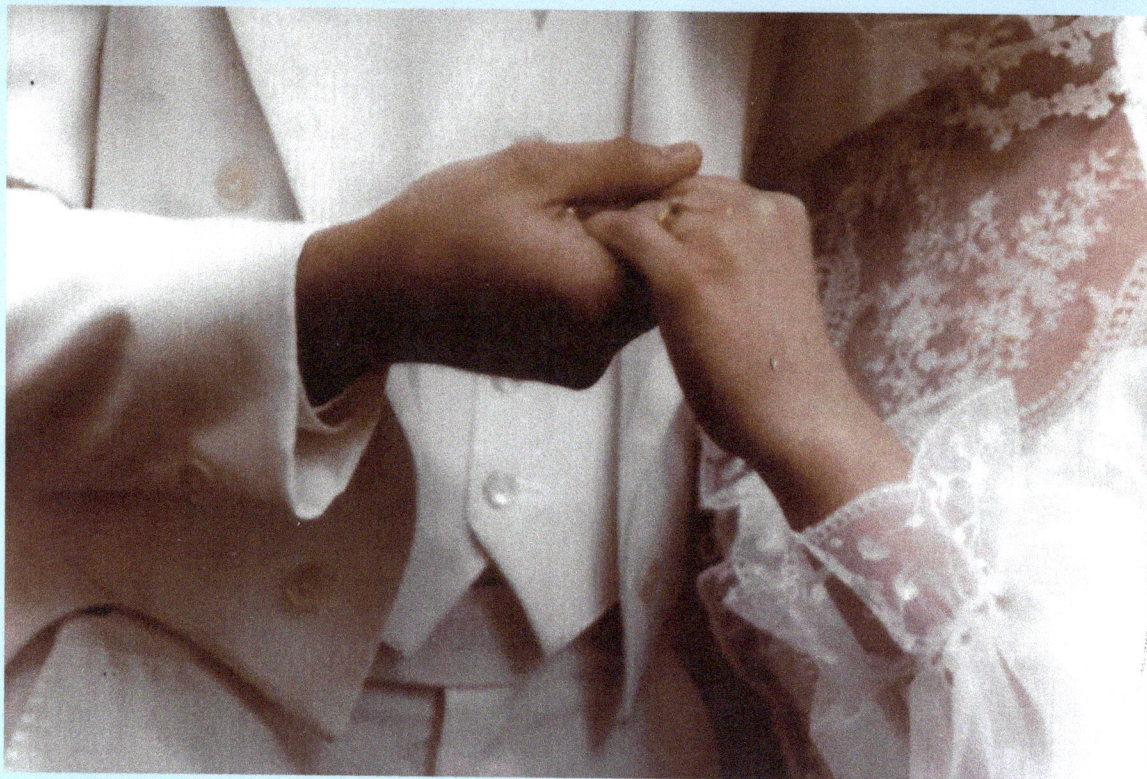

Marriage

1 Corinthians 13:4–8 has been a marriage text for many years. However, many couples who have heard that text on their wedding day are now divorced. Why do marriages fail?

Let's read the text, and ask ourselves if we could live by what St. Paul is saying. Another question is maybe even a more difficult one: In this "I" "I" "I" and "Me" "Me" "Me" world, can two people truly live by this text? Are there too many situations that can't be resolved? Are there bad habits that can't be corrected? What really makes a perfect marriage? Is there a perfect marriage?

Some do say that opposites are attracted to each other. Some believe it is a mystery that attracts two people to fall in love. We know it wasn't Cupid that shot an arrow!

I believe God has a hand as to whom we meet and fall in love with. We might say that it was a coincidence that we met him or her, but there is no coincidence with God. God created Adam, and then He created Eve. There are two important truths regarding marriage, and both truths are found in the very first book of the Bible. Genesis.

The first truth is that ordained marriage was instituted by God in The Garden of Eden. God created man and woman, and instructed that the two shall become 'one'!

In Genesis 2: 21-24 we read, "So the Lord God caused a deep sleep to fall upon the man, and he slept; then He took one of his ribs, and closed up the flesh at that place. And the Lord God fashioned into a woman the rib which He had taken from the man, and brought her to the man."

And the man said, "This is now bone of my bones, and flesh of my flesh; she shall be called Woman, because she was taken out of Man. For this cause a man shall leave his father and his mother, and shall cleave to his wife; and they shall become one flesh; consequently they are no longer two, but one flesh. What therefore God has joined together, let no man separate."

The second truth is that this is the way God wanted it then, and He still wants it for mankind today; only a marriage between a man and a woman. This is where 'social issues' surface again; 'man's ways are contrary to God's ways.'

There is a warning in 2 Timothy: 3-4: "For the time will come when they will not endure sound doctrine, but wanting to have their ears tickled, they will accumulate for themselves teachers in accordance to their own desires; and will turn away their ears from the truth, and will turn aside to myths."

I think of true love as an 'invisible thread,' and that is what keeps two people bonded as husband and wife. I heard once that 'the bedroom' is only 10 percent; it is the 90 percent that takes work. And the 90 percent is the communication, the sharing, deeply caring for each other's needs, and submitting (some do not like the word submit; even want it omitted from the marriage ceremony). If we deeply love, talk, share, and care, we won't have a problem with the word submit. Husbands and wives should be best friends.

There are, however, 'best friends' just living together, and raising their children in an unmarried household. Whatever their reasons, they are contrary to God's Will, and this is another one of those 'socially accepted choices' that people make. My one grandfather had an interesting cliché regarding an unmarried man and woman living together. He said, "Why buy the cow, when the milk is free?"

Jesus offered The Samaritan woman at the well Living Water, because He knew all about her five previous husbands, and that she was now living with a man that was not her husband. The woman believed as she said to Jesus, "I know that the Messiah is coming (He who is called Christ) when that One comes, He will declare all things to us." The woman went to the city, and told everyone, "Come see a man who told me all the things that I have done." Did she change her way of living? Only God knows, but we know she had found her Savior.

In a similar way, as Jesus confronted her about her lifestyle, so He confronts us about the life we are living, and the choices we make. There are commands in the Bible regarding intimacy that seem a bit too difficult for modern-day people to abide by. Hebrews 13:4 reads, "Let marriage be held in honor among all, and let the marriage bed be undefiled; for fornicators and adulterers God will judge."

1 Corinthians 7:1-4 reads, "It is good for a man not to touch a woman, but because of immoralities, let each man have his own wife, and let each woman have her own husband. Let the husband fulfill his duty to his wife, and likewise also the wife to her husband. The wife does not have authority over her own body, but the husband does; and likewise also the husband does not have authority over his body, but the wife does."

Will skies always be sunny? Will there be 'storms' in a marriage? Can we go through an entire calendar year without storms caused by weather conditions? The storms of a marriage can be very severe, but with deep rooted love, that 'invisible thread', will not break, and the marriage will survive. A marriage can be reconciled even if there is infidelity when there is complete repentance, and saying the most difficult words in the English language, "I'm sorry, please forgive me!" by the one, and complete forgiveness by the other. Sadly, though, many times we hear, "I'll forgive, but I won't forget." That, then, is not complete forgiveness; forgetting is the most difficult part of forgiving. In Our Lord's Prayer we ask God, "Forgive us our trespasses, as we forgive those who trespass against us." If we don't forgive, then we can't receive forgiveness either.

Will there be disagreements in a marriage? Absolutely!

We need to resolve our differences in a peaceful manner. Ephesians 4: 26 tells us, "Be Angry, and yet do not sin; do not let the sun go down on your anger."

Further in 1 Corinthians 13:11 we understand the factor of maturity, and whether we have entered into marriage as mature individuals. "When I was a child, I used to speak as a child, think as a child, reason as a child; when I became a man, I did away with childish things."

It saddens me deeply that I cannot include myself among the countless married couples that have cherished their wedding vows, and have had blessed marriages.

When aged couples can no longer be intimate, they still have eyes to look at each other affectionately, hands to hold, arms to hug, and even a tender kiss now and then.

In the movie "Guess Who's Coming To Dinner", Spencer Tracy has some beautiful dialog recollecting his admiration and love as a young man for his now aged wife played in the movie by Katharine Hepburn. I am sure there are countless husbands and wives who can recall that same admiration and love from their youth, and this is when the 'invisible thread' has not become frayed or severed.

There is no better prayer to end my marriage thoughts
than with the hymn,
"Blest Be The Tie That Binds" our hearts in
Christian love;
The unity of heart and mind Is like to that above.
Before our Father's throne we pour our ardent prayers;
our fears, our hopes, our aims are one, our comforts and
our cares.
We share our mutual woes, our mutual burdens bear,
and often for each other flows the sympathizing tear.
From sorrow, toil, and pain, and sin we shall be free;
and perfect love and friendship reign through all eternity.

Suffer The Children To Come Unto Me, And Forbid Them Not.

Jesus talks a lot about children in His ministry.

First are the children that have accepted Him as their Lord and Savior. These are the people that have the faith of a child/childlike faith, and being humble as a child in understanding and believing in Him. There are many who want to interfere with, diminish, and destroy another person's faith. Jesus' warning about anyone who hinders the faith of another person is found in Matthew 18: 4-6, and Jesus refers to the person as a 'little one': "But whoever causes one of these little ones who believes in Me to stumble, it is better for him that a heavy millstone be hung round his neck, and that he be drowned in the depth of the sea."

There are many beautiful pictures of Jesus blessing little children who their mothers had brought to Him. Three gospels illustrate Jesus taking little children into His arms and blessing them.

We bring our babies to the Lord for Baptism, marking them with the Cross of Christ, and at that moment, Jesus is taking our babies unto Himself as a child of God.

We continue to bring our children to God's House, not only because He gave them to us, but only at God's House will future generations come to know Him!

At the moment of conception, God's breath has begun a life in that little embryo, and there is no question about that, even though some people cannot, or will not, accept that fact.

To date, millions of babies have been murdered through early term or late term abortion. An injection via a needle filled with poison is inserted into that tiny skull, and a God-given life has ended. In 'late term abortion' some babies have already started sucking their thumbs and are yawning.

Whatever euphemism they use, it is murder!

We are appalled, but because of the Roe vs Wade Law passed in 1973, abortion continues throughout America. Since 1973 until 2011 (the last year statics were recorded) there have been 53 million legal (legal?) abortions in those 38 years.

In 2011 alone there were 1.06 million legal abortions. Divide 1.06 million by 365 days in that year, and that is an average of 274 babies each day! This is not legal abortion; it is legal murder!

It is a disgrace to America that Pro Choice has become a political issue. Yes, some abortionists have been prosecuted, but most are not, and again, because of the law in place.

Does not the abortionist or the baby's mother know, or do they not care that our Dear Lord Jesus is standing and watching this sinful killing of babies? And as our Lord is watching, He certainly must be praying as He prayed from the cross,

60

"Father, forgive them for they do not know what they are doing."

This outright killing of babies is far worse than King Herod sending his army into Bethlehem to kill all the male children under the age of two years old in search of Baby Jesus. This was an evil and violent act carried out by King Herod against innocent children.

We hear of evil and violent acts that take place in our schools where innocent children are killed in their classrooms. We watch and pray as a nation, and well we should, when the evening news reports these horrible evil acts. We can't even imagine what parents and communities are suffering, as we cry and watch the news. Politicians are seen as they offer sympathy and condolences to parents with words which include, ..."no more birthdays, no graduations, no weddings..."

Could the nightly news report how many abortions there have been today? We do not hear about that! Is it because these little embryos have not even seen their first birthdays, and are still nameless? We must always grieve for the violence directed to innocent school children, but we also need to grieve for our nation for allowing the slaughter of unborn babies.

This is another one of those 'choice matters' opinions, allowing people to think, "It is my body, and I can do with it whatever I want." Perhaps we may want to ask God if that is what He would want us to do.

Treasure each pregnancy; it is a gift from God! God has a purpose for that little embryo. There are no illegitimate babies; only illegitimate parents. My one grandmother used to say, "If you don't want to get pregnant, keep both feet in a bucket."

Holding your newborn in your arms for the first time is breathtaking! You look at those little fingers and toes, and you see a miracle in your arms. And that little miracle not only belongs to you, but to God. You along with God gave your baby life. God has given you a miracle, but also a responsibility.

Only you can nourish your child with food and love, and watch your little miracle grow. You can experience the joy of hearing their first words, watching those first teeth appear, and how precious to see those wobbly first steps that are attempted by your little child.

Never neglect in nourishing your children's souls. It will never be too early to sing a lullaby to your baby, and no hymn is more beautiful than "Jesus Loves Me."

"Jesus loves me, this I know, for the Bible tells me so. Little ones to Him belong; they are weak, but He is strong. Yes, Jesus loves me. Yes, Jesus loves me. Yes, Jesus loves me. The Bible tells me so."

And again, it is never too early to tell your child the beautiful story about Baby Jesus. Children are fascinated by babies. Children like to watch babies, and they can easily relate to them. Perhaps they have a new baby brother or sister, or someone in the family has a new baby.

For many children, Christmas is only a gift receiving experience, and the more gifts the merrier, but they do not know about Baby Jesus. Is this the children's fault? We know the answer. Either the children's parents or some generation in the past has failed to share the story of Baby Jesus with their children. When children cannot yet comprehend the Bible, we can purchase some wonderfully written children's books that are illustrated and tell the Christmas Story of Baby Jesus.

What about Santa Claus? Absolutely, we need Santa in the picture, and parents always enjoy watching to see how their little ones will react to seeing Santa Claus for the first time.

Then comes the anticipation of children to see what Santa has left under the Christmas Tree for them to open on Christmas Morning. Yes, Santa Claus and the gifts received are all a part of the Christmas fun, but without knowing Baby Jesus, Christmas is only a short-lived experience for children.

Christmas sometimes isn't as much fun for adults as it is for children. When we feel overwhelmed with all we need to do, and how much Christmas may cost us, we may consider just closing our eyes for a moment, and think about 'taking that long journey with Mary and Joseph to Bethlehem, and see that 'Baby' in the manger as our 'Beautiful Savior.'

For me, the Christmas season begins after an Advent Worship Service. I retrieve twelve years of Christmas concert tape cassettes which were always given to each of us by our choir director. Those arrangements bring back many treasured memories. I like one arrangement in particular that has a gospel swing melody which is entitled, "Jesus What A Wonderful Child." While listening to the tapes, I start decorating, and the most enjoyable part of decorating for Christmas is putting up my Nativity scene. My Nativity scene is white porcelain, and one Christmas many, many years ago, little granddaughters were playing with it, and one of Mary's hands was broken off, and because I couldn't find it, I couldn't glue Mary's hand back on. Because it

was an accident, we won't mention names, and since a popular phrase says, "What Happens at Grandma's House, Stays at Grandma's House." Each Christmas, Mary was always present, but with one hand missing; no one noticed, nor did anyone ever mention it.

A couple of years ago, I was amazed to discover an identical Mary in a resale shop. I did purchase my discovery, but I didn't have the heart to discard my original Mary; just keep her wrapped in tissue paper with the other figurines.

Allow your children to help when putting up a Nativity Scene, while you tell 'the story.' We sing a favorite Christmas hymn, and it is one of the first cherished

Christmas hymns that children can relate to: "Away In A Manger, no crib for His bed; the Little Lord Jesus laid down His sweet head. The stars in the sky looked down where He lay; the little Lord Jesus asleep on the hay. The cattle are lowing, the baby awakes, but little Lord Jesus no crying He makes. I love You Lord Jesus; look down from the sky, and stay by my cradle till morning is light."

I pray that you will be a blessing to your children, and that your children will come to know, to treasure, and be able to share the beautiful Christmas story with their children. Then your children will be a blessing to you, and we can sing the final verse:

"Be near me Lord Jesus, I ask Thee to stay close by me forever and love me, I pray. Bless all the dear children in Your tender care, and fit us for heaven to live with You there." Amen.

My wish for you and all generations to come:
A Blessed Christmas Always!

The Journey / The Gates

Modern technology has provided us with a GPS in our cars; I'm not sure what the letters stand for, but let's just use the phrase, "Getting Places Strategically." This device is a road map with directions allowing us to get where we want to go.

Actually, I still prefer the paper version of maps, and my preference dates back to 1972 when I became a District Sales Manager for a corporate company. GPS devices weren't in existence, and I remember receiving boxes of maps for townships, villages, and cities for one half of a county, plus one major city. I learned very quickly how not to get lost, get to appointments on time, and ensure that each person on my sales force had an accurate sales territory.

We have no intentions of getting lost, but sometimes we just do. And, sometimes we take a wrong road deliberately, and may encounter a problem. Let me share an example.

In 1989 (GPS devices weren't in

existence then either), I mapped out a route from Wisconsin to Florida. The route consisted of a stop in Memphis to visit Graceland, and then on to New Orleans. Out of New Orleans there was a deliberate change made to the route. This deliberate change to the route could have proved very dangerous. We drove down a long dirt road through dense overgrown trees, which reminded me of a green tunnel, leading to an old weathered looking shack at the end of the road. Left alone in the car for over an hour, I feared ending up in a bayou swamp! With some 'prayer time' and a sign of relief, it was back on the mapped route, and on to Florida.

A GPS or an 'old fashioned' paper road map can usually give us great directions, and we reach our destinations. What route do we use for 'this journey through life'? Jesus tells us about two routes; He refers to them as gates. The wide gate, and the narrow gate.

The Wide Gate: The way is broad, and it is when we allow ourselves to be conformed to the world by saying, "Everybody is doing it." "I am my own person, and if it feels good; do it." And we have all heard, "When in Rome, do as the Romans do." But Jesus says in Matthew 7:13: "The way is broad that leads to destruction, and many are those who enter by it." In other words, Jesus is telling us that just because everyone is doing it doesn't make it right. By conforming to the world, we may be more popular, but is it contrary to God's word? Sometimes our habits, deeds, and language are not pleasing to God, and they can distort our character as a caring and sincere Christian.

Will the love of our possessions and wealth lead us down that 'wide way?' The Bible does not tell us that possessions and wealth are sinful, but we read in Psalm 62:10, "If riches increase, do not set your heart upon them." Jesus told His disciples in Mark 10:24, "It is easier for a camel to go through the eye of a needle than for a rich man to enter the kingdom of God." And, in 1 Timothy 6:7–10 we read, "For we have brought nothing into the world, so we cannot take anything out of it either.

If we have food and covering with these we shall be content. But those who want to get rich fall into temptation and a snare and many foolish and harmful desires which plunge men into ruin and destruction. For the love of money is a root of all sorts of evil, and some longing for it have wandered away from the faith, and have pierced themselves with many a pang."

The Narrow Gate: The way is small, and it is when we can live in the world, but not allow ourselves to be conformed to the world or what is contrary to God's word. In Matthew 7: 14, Jesus tells us, "For the gate is small, and way is narrow that leads to life, and few are those who find it."

I heard an interesting comparison once; a fish that spends its entire life in salty sea water still requires salt to make it tasty. If God can allow a fish to remain salt-free in salty seawater, can He not help us overcome the things of the world that will cause us to deliberately change course or stray from the mapped out route that is God's command and will for us? St. Paul wrote to the Romans about just that in Romans 12:2: "And do not be conformed to this world, but be transformed by the renewing of your mind, that you may prove what the will of God is; that which is good and acceptable, and perfect."

Even though we are only pilgrims here journeying to our Heavenly Home, we will have fears, doubts, and problems journeying through the Narrow Gate.

There is a prayerful hymn to keep us from deliberately taking a wrong route. "Lord Jesus You Shall Be My Song, As I journey." In the last verse we sing, "I fear in the dark, and the doubt of my journey, but courage will come with the sound of Your steps by my side, and with all of the family You saved by Your love, we'll sing to Your dawn at the end of our journey."

Another hymn begins with, "Guide Me Ever, Great Redeemer, pilgrim through this barren land. I am weak, but You are mighty; hold me with Your powerful hand."

"In the holy mountain of the Lord"
Heaven

Throughout the Bible, we hear God's promises about new heavens and a new earth. From Isaiah 65: 17 God tells us, "For I create new heavens and a new earth; And the former things shall not be remembered or come to mind." In 1 Corinthians 2: 9 we read, "Things which eye has not seen, and ear has not heard, and which have not entered the heart of man, All that God has prepared for those who love Him." And in 2 Peter 3: 13 we are told, "But according to His promise we are looking for new heavens and a new earth, in which righteousness dwells."

But we, mere man, still wonder what heaven will truly be like. The Apostle John may have had a glimpse as we read the book of Revelations. Much of Revelations is difficult to understand, and we are not sure about streets of gold, and pearly gates.

In Chapter 7 of Revelations, verses 9-17, there is an account regarding "A Multitude from the Tribulation." "It was a multitude that no one could count, from every nation, and all tribes and peoples and tongues standing before the Lamb clothed in white robes, and palm branches were in their hands; and they cry out with a loud voice, saying, "Salvation to our God, who sits on the throne, and to the Lamb." They fell on their faces, and worshiped God. It was asked, "These who are clothed in white, who are they, and from where have they come?" It was answered, "These are the ones who have come out of the great tribulation, and they have washed their robes and made them white in the blood of the Lamb." We believe that this multitude described could very well be the faithful followers of Christ Jesus, and are those that have accepted Jesus as their Lord and Savior; believed that they are saved by the blood that Jesus shed on the cross, took on their sins, and died to sin in their place.

There has been great tribulation in the past, is still here today, and tribulation will continue until the end of time/our time here on earth, and I pray that I will be numbered in 'that multitude', and I pray that you, my dear grandchildren, and generations to come will be in that multitude as well.

And what do we read from the Bible regarding non believing family members that refuse to accept Jesus as their Lord and Savior, want nothing to do with church, and shun God's Holy Law.

First and foremost we can't judge anyone; that is up to God, because only God can look into hearts and minds. We should only love and encourage our loved ones to seek the Lord. And, we pray that it not be that their names be blotted out of the 'Book of Life' as we read in Deuteronomy 9:14 and Psalm 69:28. God tells us that we will not remember any family members who may not be with us in heaven.

Jesus tells us in John 14:1-3, "Let not your heart be troubled; believe in God, believe also in Me. In My Father's house are many dwelling places; If it were not so, I would have told you; for I go to prepare a place for you. And if I go and prepare a place for you, I will come again, and receive you to Myself; that where I am, there you may be also."

Chapter 21 of Revelations, verses 1-9, also speaks about 'The New Heaven and The New Earth.' Perhaps "The New Earth" is The Garden of Eden where God created Adam and Eve to live forever, and not to sin. Wherever the New Earth will be, we will live eternally with God.

"In The Holy Mountain Of The Lord" is another of my favorite songs while singing with a church choir. The choral arrangement depicts 'the peace' of the Kingdom of God, and certainly must have been taken from Isaiah 11:6-9 as "The wolf will dwell with the lamb, And the leopard will lie down with the kid, And the calf and young lion and fatling together; And a little boy will lead them. Also, the cow and the bear will graze; Their young will lie down together; And the lion will eat straw with the

ox. And the nursing child will play by the hole of the cobra, And the weaned child will put his hand on the viper's den. They shall do no evil or harm in all My Holy Mountain, says the Lord."

Will there really be animals in heaven that we need not fear? Any animals? And, how about my favorite at the zoo? The giraffe! At the zoo, the giraffes appear so docile; like you could just walk up to them and pet them. Could we pet such animals in heaven? Unknown at this time! Of course, we still may have some apprehension about petting those beautiful lions, tigers, or sleek black leopards!

Also, unknown at this time is when our earthly life will cease, and when God will call us to Himself. That year, that day, or that hour is only known by God.

On my day, I picture Jesus walking toward me as He walked toward the Apostle John on the Isle of Patmos. Jesus already knows what my prayer and song will be even if I am not of sound mind or physically unable to speak.

A beautiful hymn!
"Precious Lord, Take My Hand
lead me on, let me stand.
I am tired, I am weak, I am worn.
Through the storm, through the night,
lead me on to the light, take my hand,
Precious Lord, lead me 'Home'."

Be Aware Of False Prophets

In Matthew 24:24 Jesus warns us, "For false Christs and false prophets will arise and will show great signs and wonders, so to mislead, if possible, even the elect. And again in Matthew 7:15 Jesus tells us, "Beware of false prophets, who come to you in sheep's clothing, but inwardly are ravenous wolves."

And when false prophets surface they will try to convince people that the Old Testament is no longer relevant, past history, and what was spoken and warned against by the prophets in the Old Testament cannot be taken seriously because times have changed , and those laws don't meet today's standards. Isn't that interesting? The Ten Commandment were given to Moses by God Himself in the second book (Exodus) of the Old Testament.

Are the Ten Commandments then no longer to be considered relevant?

This is a great time to give the account of the Ten Commandments. Picture Moses standing in the presence of God, and actually speaking to God. Exodus 31:18 reads, "And when God had finished speaking with Moses upon Mount Sinai, He gave Moses the two tables of the testimony, tablets of stone, written by the finger of God."

As we read the following two chapters, Exodus 32 and 33, we learn that the children of Israel felt Moses, and possibly God, too,

had abandoned them, because Moses had been up on Mount Sinai for 40 days. They took it upon themselves to make a golden calf which they actually started to worship. And what did Moses do? Exodus 32:19 tells us, "And it came about, as Moses came near the camp, that he saw the calf and the dancing; and Moses' anger burned and he threw the tablets from his hands and shattered them at the foot of the mountain."

Moses, then, took the calf which the Children of Israel had made, and burned it with fire, and ground it to powder, scattered it over the surface of water, and made the sons of Israel drink it. You may think that God said, "Oops! Guess I have to write those commandments again." But, God did not say that. God was even angrier than Moses could think about being; God wanted to destroy the Children of Israel. God told Moses the people had corrupted themselves, and had become an obstinate people. Then God told Moses, "Now let Me alone, that My anger may burn against them, and that I may destroy them."

Reading the conversation between Moses and God in chapters 32 and 33, we learn that Moses interceded for the people, and asks God if He brought them out of slavery from the Pharaoh of Egypt, through the parted waters of the Red Sea only to now destroy them? Moses, also, asks God if He had forgotten His promises to Abraham, Isaac, and Jacob? And, Moses reminded God that this nation is 'Thy people.'

In Exodus 33:17 we read that God did change His mind, "And God said to Moses, I will do this of which you have spoken; for you have found favor in My sight, and I have known you by name." Then Exodus 34:1 tells us, now the Lord said to Moses, "Cut out for yourself two stone tablets like the former ones, and I will write on the tablets the words that were on the former tablets which you shattered."

The Ten Commandments are and always will be God's Law. Irrelevant? Never!

What did Jesus say about the Law and the Prophets? In Matthew 5:17–18 He tells us, "Do you think that I came to abolish the Law and the Prophets; I did not come to abolish, but to fulfill. For truly I say to you, until heaven and earth pass away, not the smallest letter or stroke shall pass away from the Law, until all is accomplished." Jesus did exactly as He had said; He fulfilled the Law perfectly, and He is the Messiah that the Prophets had prophesied would redeem people from their sins.

Beware! Someday false prophets will come forth to say that the New Testament is 'past history,' 'not relevant,' or 'doesn't conform with today's standards.' I can't remember if it was when I was in 7th or 8th grade at our parochial school, but it was requested of our class to memorize Jesus' Sermon On The Mount which is found in Matthew chapters 5, 6, and 7. (We added the verses up in school, and I just did the math again; 111 verses!). The Sermon On The Mound is also referred to as The Beatitudes, and throughout the sermon, Jesus more fully explains the Ten Commandments, and places more emphasis on how to pray, personal relationships, dealing with anxiety, living in the world, but not conforming to the world. Could it be that this beloved sermon by Jesus could, too, someday be considered irrelevant?

In 1 Timothy 6:3, St. Paul warns us what false prophets will try to do, and we read, "If anyone advocates a different doctrine, and does not agree with sound words of our Lord Jesus Christ, and with the doctrine conforming to godliness, he is conceited and understands nothing; but he has a morbid interest in controversial questions and disputes about words out of which arise envy, strife, abusive language, evil suspicions and constant friction between men of depraved mind and deprived of the truth who suppose that godliness is a means of gain." And in Galatians 1:6-10, St. Paul speaks to the Galatians, and tells us today, "I am amazed that you are so quickly deserting Him who called you by the grace of Christ, for a different gospel; which is really not another; only some who are disturbing you, and want to distort the gospel of Christ. But even though we, or an angel from heaven should preach to you a gospel contrary to that which we have preached to you, let him be accused. As we have said before, so I say again now, if any man is preaching to you a gospel contrary to that which you received, let him be accused. For am I now seeking the favor of men, or of God? Or am I striving to please men? If I am trying to please men, I would not be a bond-servant of Christ."

This is where St. Paul would, again, say that those that cannot accept The Law of the Old Testament and the Gospel of the New Testament as written, and live their lives by it, have a quarrel with God.

There are two accounts that false prophets should familiarize themselves with, and we find the first account in 1 Corinthians 6:9-11: "Or do you not know that the unrighteous shall not inherit the kingdom of God? Do not be deceived; neither fornicators, nor idolaters, nor adulterers, nor effeminates, nor homosexuals, nor thieves, nor the covetous, nor drunkards, nor revilers, nor swindlers, shall inherit the kingdom of God."

But then St. Paul adds, "And such were some of you; but you were washed, but you were sanctified, but you were justified in the name of the Lord Jesus Christ, and in the Spirit of our God." And In the second account we read from 1 Timothy 1:8-11. St. Paul talks about the Law and says, "But we know that the Law is good, if one uses it lawfully, realizing the fact that the Law is not made for a righteous man, but for those who are lawless and rebellious, for the ungodly and sinners, which we are, for the unholy and profane, for those who kill their fathers and mothers, for murderers and immoral men and homosexuals and kidnappers and liars and perjurers, and whatever else is contrary to sound teaching, according to the glorious gospel of the blessed God, with which I have been entrusted."

There is one thing that false prophets can never deny, and that is that Jesus did truly exist.

No question about that; that is history!

What they are trying to convince people of is that Jesus was only a teacher, a friend, a law abiding person, and a good person. But a God? False prophets will try to convince people further that a God can't become human; well, our God did! The birth of Jesus and His birth place had been prophesized in the Old Testament, and we find that in Micah 5:2, "But as for you, Bethlehem Ephrathah, Too little to be among the clans of Judah, From you, Bethlehem, One will go forth for Me to be ruler in Israel. His goings forth are from long ago, From the days of eternity." In Isaiah 7:14 we read, "Therefore the Lord Himself will give you a sign: Behold a virgin will be with child and bear a son, and she will call His name Immanuel," which translated means, "God with us."

The Annunciation to the Virgin Mary is recorded In Luke 1:26-38. An angel visited Mary and told her she had found favor with God, and that she would conceive and bear a son. In Luke 1:34-35, Mary said to the angel, "How can this be since I am a virgin?" The angel answered and said to her, "The Holy Spirit will come upon you, and the power of the Most High will over-shadow you; and for that reason the Holy offspring shall be called the Son of God." Jesus truly did join humankind as a baby born of the Virgin Mary. Yes, He was a teacher, a friend to sinners, and he obeyed not only man's law, but obeyed and spoke of God's Law. But all the while Jesus was True God.

And, then, again false prophets will ask, "But a God? A God cannot die."

Our God did indeed die, and He died the most despicable cruel death of that era; crucifixion. Our Dear Lord and Savior, Jesus Christ, took all the sins of the entire world to that cross; the sins of all those who have lived and have died, the sins of us living today, and the sins of those who aren't even born yet.

How is that possible? The most beautiful verse in the Bible explains it: John 3:16 reads, "For God so loved the world, that He gave His only gotten Son, that whoever believes in Him should not perish, but have eternal life." The following verses are thought provoking for us, and perhaps someday, false prophets, too, may truly believe what John continues to say in John 3:17-21: "For God did not send His Son into the world to judge the world, but that the world should be saved through Him. Anyone who believes in Him is not judged; anyone who does not believe has been judged already, because they have not believed in the name of the only begotten Son of God. And this is the judgment, that the light is come into the world, and people loved the darkness rather than light; for their deeds were evil. For everyone who does evil hates the light, and does not come to the light, lest their deeds be exposed. But they who practice the truth come to the light, that their deeds may be manifested as having been wrought in God."

False Prophets can't fathom Jesus as True God being in the tomb on Holy Saturday, descending into hell, and declaring victory over Satan, thereby fulfilling His Almighty Mission by dying for the sins of the world, and destroying the forces of Satan. The ravenous wolves in the wild want to devour your flesh, but those ravenous wolves, the False Prophets in sheep's clothing, in the second verse at the beginning of this message do want to devour your soul.

Jesus overcame death with His Glorious Resurrection on the third day just as He had said He would.

We sing "Hallelujah! Jesus Lives," and "Jesus Christ Is Risen Today." But before we sing those songs, let's go back to the tomb where Jesus' body had been placed after He was taken down from the cross. Pilate had ordered soldiers to block the tomb with a huge stone, and also posted guards so that Jesus' followers couldn't take His body, and then say that He had arisen.

Early, at dawn, on the first day of the week, Mary Magdalene and other women who had prepared spices were going to the tomb. On the way the thought probably came to them regarding the huge stone. They probably said to each other, "What are we thinking; who is going to roll away the stone so we can anoint Jesus' body?"

We know that when the women arrived at the tomb, the huge stone had already been rolled away, and as they were standing there weeping and looking into the tomb they saw two angels in white sitting, one at the head, and one at the feet where Jesus' body had been laying.

And the angels asked, "Why are you weeping?" Mary replied, "Because they have taken my Lord, and I do not know where they have laid Him." Mary turned and saw a man, but did not know that is was Jesus, and thinking it was a gardener, she asked, "Sir, if you have carried Him away, tell me where you have laid Him."

Jesus softly spoke her name, "Mary," and she recognized Him. Can we even imagine how quickly her tears of sorrow were now turning to tears of joy? And that joy must have filled Mary's heart.

Just two days earlier, Mary had stood with Jesus's mother beneath the cross, and had watched her Savior die in agony as His hands and feet were nailed to the cross, the crown of thorns piercing His head, which must have caused blood to run down His face, and the piercing of His side that had pronounced Him dead. Now, here He was standing before her, and it was as the angels had said, "He is not here, He is risen!" Mary ran announcing to the disciples, "I have seen the Lord!"

Now, with Mary, we sing all those beautiful Easter songs, including the song of Job, "I know That My Redeemer Lives".

St. Paul couldn't have spoken it more beautifully than he did in 1 Corinthians 15: "If Jesus Christ had not risen, preaching is in vain, our faith is vain and worthless, and we are still in our sins. But Christ has been raised from the dead, and thanks be to God who gives us the victory through our Lord Jesus Christ."

After Jesus's command to His disciples that they be His witnesses to the remotest part of the earth, and make disciples of all nations, baptizing in the name of the Father, and of the Son, and of the Holy Spirit, we have the account of Jesus's Ascension in Act 1:9-11: "And after He had said these things, He was lifted up while they were looking on, and a cloud received Him out of their sight. And as they were gazing intently into the sky while He was departing, behold two men in white clothing stood beside them; and they said, "Men of Galilee, why do you stand looking into the sky? This Jesus, who now has been taken up from you into heaven, will come in just the same way as you have watched Him go into heaven."

A noted commentator Paul Harvey used to end a commentary saying, "Now, you know the rest of the story!"

But this is not the 'rest of this story!'

False prophets need to know that "The Best of Jesus' Story Is Yet To Come"!

"Evil Under The Sun"

An Agatha Christie novel, and a movie by the same title.

The evil under the sun played out in the movie doesn't even compare to the tremendous evil that is gripping the earth in this day and age. (You might just want to catch this movie for ladies' fashions; outstanding and gorgeous.)

With each new sunrise, we need to take heed as we read in 1 Peter 5:8-10, "Be of sober spirit, be on the alert, your adversary, the devil, prowls about like a roaring lion seeking someone to devour. But resist him, firm in your faith, knowing that the same experiences of suffering are being endured by your brethren who are in the world. And after you have suffered for a little while, the God of all grace who called you to His eternal glory in Christ will Himself perfect, confirm, strengthen, and establish you."

Many people throughout the world, and right here in America, have experienced the most horrible evil acts because of the devil. The devil isn't done with the world; he has his advocates and ambassadors, and they are alive and well among us waiting and wanting to devour our souls.

There is a movie in which the devil has taken over the entire being of a man, and in the movie the man enjoys being the devil's advocate. Of course it is a movie, but the fact of the matter is that it represents how the devil can totally and completely take over a person's life when allowed. There is an interesting ending to the movie in that the devil appears as a very handsome gentleman, and therein lays the temptation; who can resist such a handsome man? He will undoubtedly find his next victim.

The devil doesn't care about the ones already in his flock; he seeks out and wants the ones who are faithful to God, namely us. If the devil can weaken our faith, and make us vulnerable to temptation, he has succeeded in his efforts. When the devil enters the thoughts and hearts of men, women, and even children, evil deeds are put in motion.

First thoughts, then words, and then deeds.

Thoughts plot evil. Words put things in motion to carry out plans, and then deeds are the physical force which is the ultimate weapon to carry out that first evil thought.

Sometimes no physical deed may be needed to injure another person or even a loved one; evil and hateful thought-out words can be very disparaging and damaging when spoken to or about and against others. We are warned about our tongue in James 3:7-8, "For every species of beasts and birds, of reptiles and creatures of the sea is tamed by the human race. But no one can tame the tongue; it is a restless evil and full of deadly poison."

There is another evil that we are seeing and hearing about, and it is regarding individuals who want to obliterate every symbol that pertains to God and Christianity from the landscape across America, and further, to abolish every word that pertains to God and Christianity from our vocabulary. The devil is doing a great job through these individuals to accomplish both of these tasks.

In Matthew 13:24-30 and 36-43, Jesus tells us about the evil among us: "The one who sows the good seed is the Son of Man, and the field is the world; and as for the good seed, these are the sons of the Kingdom, and the weeds are the sons of the evil one. And the enemy who sowed weeds is the devil. When the good seed sprang up and bore grain, then the weeds became evident also. And the slaves of the landowner came and said to him, "Sir, did you not sow good seeds in your field? How then is it that there are weeds? The landowner replied, "An enemy has done this!" The slaves asked if they should gather the weeds, but the landowner said, "No, for while you pull out the weeds, you may root up the wheat with them. Allow both to grow together until the harvest, and in the time of the harvest I will tell the reapers to first gather up the weeds, bind them in bundles, and burn them up. Gather the wheat into my barn."

And so it will be until the end of the world, we will need to live among the evil under the sun, the harvest is the end of the age, and the reapers will be the angels.

St. Peter tell us in 1 Peter 3:12, "For the eyes of the Lord are upon the righteous, and His ears attend to their prayer, but the face of the Lord is against those who do evil." St. James encourages us in James 4:7, "Submit therefore to God. Resist the devil, and he will flee from you."

It is very fitting to end this message with the third verse from the hymn, "A Mighty Fortress Is Our God":

"Though hordes of devils fill the land, all threatening to devour us, we tremble not, unmoved we stand; they cannot overpower us. Let this world's tyrant rage; in battle we'll engage! The devil's might is doomed to fail; God's judgment must prevail! One little word subdues him!"

On Eagle's Wings

The eagle is the most majestic bird in the sky; the very symbol of America. I once watched an eagle feed its young through a telescope, and it was a heartwarming thing to see.

I've heard that one politician believes that the eagle is another reason for global warming, and should possibly become extinct. Really? Could it be that this majestic bird which God created should now become extinct? May God intervene so that this does not happen!

God, also, created those little annoying gnats that can get through a window screen during the summer; how about putting some legislature in place to make them extinct?

In Matthew 10:29-30, Jesus tells us that no sparrow will fall to the ground unless it is God's will. Will God not be saddened by the destruction of eagles?

Even Isaiah refers to eagles when encouraging us to wait for the Lord to gain new strength. Isaiah 40:30-31 reads, "Though youths grow weary and tired, And vigorous young men stumble badly, Yet those who wait for the Lord will gain new strength; They will mount up with wings like eagles. They will run and not get tired, They will walk and not become weary."

When we stumble and fall, I'm not talking about falling off of our bike, or stumbling on the playground and skinning our knee, and neither is Isaiah. Of course there probably weren't any bicycles in Isaiah's day. At least there isn't any mention of them.

Isaiah is talking about stumbling and falling on the 'playground of life.' And when we stumble and fall on this 'playground of life,' we need God's majestic power to bear us up!

There is a beautiful song, "You Who Dwell in the Shelter of the Lord" (sometimes entitled "On Eagle's Wings"), and the Refrain goes like this:

"And I will raise you up on eagle's wings, bear you on the breath of dawn, make you to shine like the sun, and hold you in the palm of My hand."

I encourage you to read Psalm 103. It is a Psalm of praise to God for all His tender mercies toward us. Verse 5 reads, "Who satisfies your years with good things, so your youth is renewed like the eagle."

God Bless America

When Kate Smith sang "God Bless America," she sang it as though she were praying it. We could hear it in her voice as she sang, "God Bless America, land that I love, stand beside her, and guide her with the light that shines from above..."

You may not know who Kate Smith was, but you could Google her. Maybe there is a recording of her singing this hymn.

America has been blessed with prosperity in many areas of industry, agriculture, medical inventions too numerous to mention, and many businesses and corporations through entrepreneurial individuals.

Because of our prosperity, Americans have a gracious, benevolent spirit in charitable giving, and in offering aid of goods and money here in America, and to countries when devastated by severe weather conditions and catastrophes. Every day we need to give thanks to God for our own personal blessings which He has bestowed on us.

Let us never forget to thank God for our strong Armed Forces. America's Armed Forces have befriended, defended, and supported ally nations around the world.

Many men and women have given their lives as an ultimate sacrifice to keep America safe and our freedom secure.

At the back of my "Portals of Prayers," which is a daily devotional book, I always pray the prayer for our Armed Forces. In our family there have been ten men who have served in our Armed Forces. Four served in active duty, and all returned home without harm or injury; what an outstanding blessing from God. I remember active duty very well; I gave birth to Sarah in an Army hospital. One woman in our family served with The American Red Cross, and her daughter served in the Peace Corps.

First and foremost, (and I say this now because of the paragraph which follows), we have had the wonderful freedom to worship the God on which America was founded.

With anger and determination in his voice, an individual from a Middle East country was seen threatening America that they would not stop until their flag would be flying over our White House. We need to pray very sincerely that this will never happen. Looking at a map, one can clearly see that some Middle East countries aren't even half the size of the state of Texas. How is it that such a small nation can impose such a devastating threat to us? And, the nation imposing such a threat does not believe in the God which America was founded on. Our God, whom they don't believe in, sees all, and in God's own good time He will prevail over evil. I definitely urge you to read Psalm 53, which is a short six verses, that begins: "The fool has said in his heart, 'There is no God.'"

Let's never forget another nationality of people, the Jewish people, who fled Europe, and especially from Germany, because Hitler wanted to exonerate the entire Jewish race. They, too, sought safe haven by coming to America. The Jewish people built their temples and synagogues, and the Christians built their cathedrals and churches. Both found work, raised their families, and both lived in harmony with each other, and more importantly have respected each other's faith.

The Christians did not find the Jewish symbols or holidays offensive, and Jewish people did not find the Christian symbols or holidays offensive. The reason for that is because both peoples are God fearing people, and neither needed to fear each other.

I once had the opportunity to be a member of an ecumenical council, and had the pleasure to meet a Jewish Rabbi. I can still remember how inspiring it was to hear him express his faith.

We hear reports that the nation of Israel is being threatened by a neighboring nation. I wholeheartedly believe that God will not allow anything to happen to the Jewish people, because they are still 'God's Chosen People.'

We should always exercise our right to vote! Not just for the Presidential elections, but also for state governor, senate, and congressional elections, which are mid-term elections. We need to educate ourselves about the candidates and what their platforms are, and keep ourselves informed concerning our state governor, senators, and congressmen, and know their track record as to how they governed. Do they govern for 'the people' or for 'their party?'

Currently there are various political parties in America, and it is confusing and alarming to see that many parties on the ballot. In my thinking that is too many, and one may wonder what party will and could be present on our ballots in the future.

Let's not just watch local news, but find cable stations that report in an unbiased and balanced manner which explains precisely what each candidate's platform is.

We can find religious cable channels which report from God's perspective.

My father would be appalled at the number of political parties on the ballot. He knew politics, and voted until his death at age 90. When he could no longer go to the polls by himself, my sister who lived nearer to him needed to obtain an absentee ballot for him.

There are some beautiful Psalms to read during an election year, and I urge you to read them. Psalms 36, 37, and 59, and then vote your conscience.

There is an alarming epidemic spreading throughout America right now, and that pertains to vile and vulgar words in our vocabulary. Every vile and vulgar word known to mankind rolls right off the tongue, and these words are being commonly used as nouns, adverbs, and adjectives. If such words can be heard in supermarkets and retail stores, they certainly must be spoken in homes. Such foul language is alarming and distasteful. Could it be another 'sign of the times' that we live in, and that these vile and vulgar words are becoming 'socially correct'? How pitiful!

When an immediate family suffers discord and friction, the family breaks apart, and love for each other is destroyed, and this is what our American family is suffering from today. We hear about all the wars on different classes of people; a 'war on the rich,' a 'war on the poor,' a 'war on women,' and tomorrow we will probably hear about a 'war on something else,' We read about exactly that in Micah 7:1-6. All these wars among ourselves are breaking up our American family, and because we are fighting from within we will destroy the love and respect that we have for each other, and America will suffer as a nation. Here are some tough questions: Who is responsible for starting all these 'wars?' Does America still present itself to the world as a Christian and a God fearing nation, and if we aren't, why aren't we? And who is responsible for that? Have we Americans not taken a firm enough stand to defend the faith that our government was founded on? Or, have we taken for granted that our government would continue to defend the faith that America was founded on? Have Americans stopped thanking God for their own and America's prosperity? Tough questions, aren't they? America certainly is in need of a Savior; Jesus, The Prince of Peace, as Micah concludes in verses 7-20.

Jesus frequently explained more fully the prophecies from the Old Testament Prophets, and in Matthew 10 Jesus expounds on what Micah had written, and Jesus talks about a sword, but He is not referring to a weapon; He is referring to the sword which is sometimes referred to in describing and being The Holy Scriptures/ The Word Of God. God's Word can cut through the hardest of hearts, can penetrate those hearts, minds, and lives to bring about a change to what is perplexing and causing suffering not just to individuals, but to nations. We are warned in

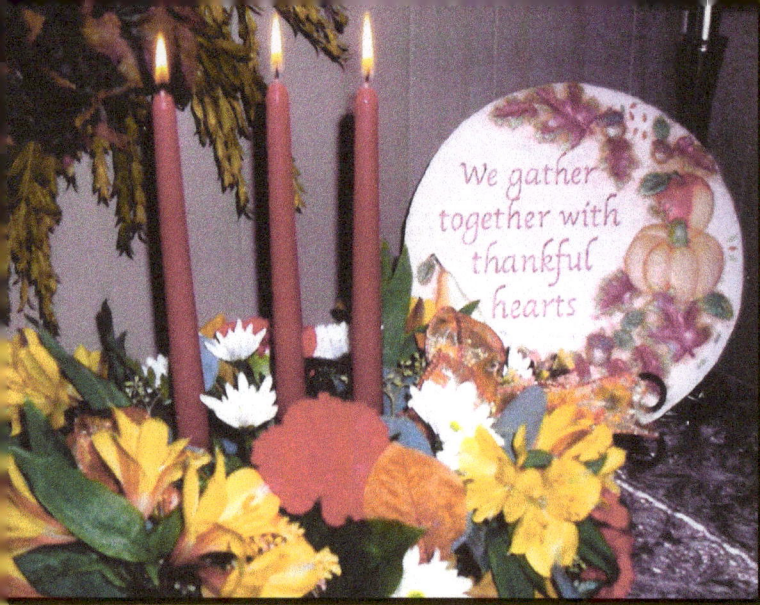

1 Corinthians 10:12, "Therefore let him who thinks he stands take heed lest he fall," and in 2 Peter 3:17, "You therefore beloved, knowing this beforehand, be on your guard lest being carried away by the error of unprincipled men, you fall from your own steadfastness." Has America left God? Perhaps America is a 'Prodigal Son' nation. If that is the case, God will welcome 'Her' back with open arms!

Psalm 33 is a psalm of praise to God as our Creator and Preserver, and in verse 12 we hear, "Blessed is the nation whose God is the Lord."

It is such a joy and a pleasure to worship God on Thanksgiving Day and sing, "Come, ye thankful people, come; Raise the song of harvest home. All be safely gathered in ere the winter storms begin. God, our maker, doth provide for our wants to be supplied. Come to God's own temple, come. Raise the song of harvest home."

Our family has a wonderful Thanksgiving Tradition. A few years ago I found a heavy cotton Thanksgiving tablecloth.. As each family arrives, each member signs their name and the date, in permanent marker, on the tablecloth. I have washed the tablecloth for nine years, and each signature is still very legible.

For some Americans, Thanksgiving Day has just become a day to get ready for, and even begin Christmas shopping. Is it that the shoppers have denied the retail employees of Thanksgiving Day? No, it is the greed of corporate retailers that have begrudged and denied their loyal employees of Thanksgiving Day.

On that First Thanksgiving Day, the Pilgrims weren't concerned about Christmas shopping; they were thankful for their first crops in the new world, and they just possibly needed to deal with a few unfriendly Indians. Have we come a long way? Or, are we becoming less and less 'thankful.' that we cannot give up an entire day out of the year to give thanks, and spend time with those we love?

There are beautiful hymns that are sung to defend our faithfulness to God, and I pray you will look for them for encouragement. One hymn is "Onward Christian Soldiers," and another is "A Mighty Fortress Is Our God."

Let's pray the last verse of another beautiful hymn entitled: "My Country 'Tis Of Thee".

"My Country 'Tis Of Thee, our father's God! To Thee, Author of liberty, To Thee I sing; Long may our land be bright, with freedom's holy light; Protect us by Thy Might, Great God, our King! Amen."

Men and women in all branches of the military have given their very lives to defend America because of their love of country, love of freedom, and love for the principles on which America was founded.

Take a walk through a Veterans Park someday, and read the names of fallen heroes; some with the same last names.

That's Entertainment

This would be an opportune place to address entertainment in America.

I'll go back to 1948; I was eight years old. My brother and I came home from school, and there was a surprise in our living room. A TV! Wow! I can still remember the first show we watched! Howdy Dowdy with Buffalo Bob, mean old Mr. Bluster, and Carrabelle the mischievous clown. I also remember Kukla, Fran, & Ollie (Kukla and Ollie were puppets, and Fran was a lady). And then there was "I Remember Mama". Let's not forget the westerns; Roy Rogers & Dale Evans, Gene Autry, and The Lone Ranger. As I grew older I enjoyed "The Voice of Firestone" which starred famous opera vocalists. I still enjoy "La Boheme"; this is the opera which Edward took Vivian to in "Pretty Woman."

Yes, we Americans like entertainment, and we could say that many entertainers have been blessed with God-given talents through their music, movies, and comedy.

To name a few comedians: Lucille Ball, Carol Burnett, Sid Ceaser & Imogene Coca, Jackie Gleason, Dean Martin & Jerry Lewis, George Burns & Gracie Allen, Bud Abbot & Lou Costilla, and Red Skelton. My grandmother Ruth enjoyed George Burns & Gracie Allen, and Groucho Marx who had a 'quiz show.'

And why do I bring attention to these particular entertainers that you, my grandchildren, have never heard of? These entertainers were not just comedians, but their talent and acting ability were always hilarious and entertaining. Their shows and skits appeared on TV on various evenings throughout the week. My father enjoyed comedy, and I remember watching many of these TV shows with him.

My father especially liked Bob Hope. Bob Hope not only appeared on TV, but he appeared in numerous movies, many of which Bing Crosby also appeared in.

Bob Hope even flew overseas to entertain our Armed Forces, and took some 'Hollywood Beauties' with him (two that I remember were Angie Dickenson and Kim Novack). What a morale booster that must have been for our dear service men and women! No one does such a patriotic mission anymore.

In listening to and watching these entertainers, we never heard an obscenity from any of them, nor did any of these entertainers ever take the Lord's name in vain. Even late night talk-show comedians like Steve Allen or Johnny Carson were not explicit in their dialog.

Present day comedians can't deliver comedy without obscene language, taking the Lord's name in vain, and some even ridicule and criticize the Christian faith. We read in Galatians 6:7, "Do not be deceived, God is not mocked."

There is one late night comedian that especially seems to enjoy ridiculing our Christian faith, and I am actually praying for him; he doesn't know it, but God does. We all know that with God nothing is impossible, and I'm thinking how great it would be if Jesus would confront this gentleman in his backstage dressing room or at an airport, and ask him as He asked Saul on the Damascus Road, "Why are you persecuting Me?" (I probably know that this scenario will not happen, but it is an interesting thought). If this gentleman would ridicule or criticize another faith or religion he would literally be reprimanded and would be taken off the air. No one is concerned about him criticizing the Christian faith.

I thoroughly enjoy watching movies; am somewhat addicted to the Hallmark Channel and American Movie Classics. My three favorite movies are "Gone With The Wind," "The Godfather," and "The Passion." I should, however, mention "Rainman." The saddest line in the movie is when Charlie asks Dr. Brunner, "Why didn't anyone ever tell me that I had a brother?"

The movie is a beautiful story about brotherly love. Dustin Hoffman is a great actor because he totally takes on the character role, and one forgets who he really is. Another such movie is "Scent Of A Woman" with Al Pacino. Again, great character role, and acting by Al Pacino. Both gentlemen totally deserve their Academy Awards! That is sheer enjoyment when an actor or an actress can take on the personality of the character role.

I do surf the cable menus, and find movies that I might like to see, but they are on pay cable channels to which I do not subscribe. Sometimes I have gone to a rental place to rent a particular movie, and sometimes I have even purchased a movie, and then I wished I hadn't, because it includes too much violence, sex, and obscenity.

I often wonder, and I would like to ask someone in the movie industry, "How much acting ability or talent is really required to make a sex scene or appear nude?" Can nothing be left to the imagination anymore?

There is a priceless old classic movie of drama and love entitled "Casablanca," and probably only a younger movie connoisseur has seen it and appreciates it. In the movie, an escape is planned from Casablanca, and Ingrid Bergman believes Humphrey Bogart will leave with her, but he has never had any intentions of leaving with her. He bids her a fond farewell and tells her, "We'll always have Paris." That statement has an emotional impact on her as you see tears running down her cheeks. There is no need for an explicit flashback of an affair that they probably had in Paris; anyone's imagination can figure it out. In the movie, "To Have and Have Not" you see Lauren Bacall's sultry look and dialog directed to Humphrey Bogart when she tells him, " Just whistle; you know how to whistle, don't you?" We can surmise what the lady's intentions are. Actors and actresses of years gone by, and many current ones as well are to be complimented, because they find it beneath their dignity to appear in the nude or take part in a sex scene. Enough said about that.

I am, many times, in hopes of enjoying a new release, and sometimes it is a huge disappointment. A latest 'new release' is "Noah," and it is just that; a huge disappointment, and more than that it is a total falsehood, and I should have placed it in the false prophet's message.

Hollywood has made some great religious movies which include "The Ten Commandments," "The Passion," and "The Robe"(even though some of "The Robe" is fictitious).

"Noah," a movie of epic proportion, is indeed a falsehood and an extreme disappointment. How could Hollywood get this movie so wrong? Answer: They didn't read the account from The Bible, or they didn't want to. It was very annoying that there was no mention of God. There was no mention of the fact that God decided to destroy all of mankind and the world except for Noah and his family because of how sinful mankind had become at that time. The movie leads you to believe that the idea of the flood was (and get this!) Noah's idea, and the only reason for the flood was to destroy mankind because man wasn't caring for the environment. Noah was even led to believe that he and his family would be the last inhabitants on the entire earth. All of it, totally annoying!! Then we see the large 'stone-like creatures' which came to life, and there was one which befriended Noah and actually helped Noah build the ark.

And lastly, an evil descendant of Cain became a stowaway on board. The Bible tells us that God closed the door to the ark. I think God would have known if there had been an evil descendant of Cain on board before He closed the door.

What they did get correct was that there was a man named Noah, there was an ark, there was a flood, and there was a dove with an olive branch in its beak. Other than those four items, the movie was totally fictitious, and an embarrassment to God.

I was waiting for the end (in more ways than one) to find out how they would interpret the rainbow. There were outstanding special effects in displaying the spectacular colors which were very vivid and evident, but the shape of the rainbow was not to be seen. I was glad I only rented it for $2.99 plus tax.

I believe Hollywood's pretense was that they just entitled the movie "Noah" to get people to theatres and entice curiosity seekers. I thank God that I know the true story of Noah, or I would have been very disillusioned. What is the moral of this? Next time there is a movie release with a Biblical title, and we aren't really sure of the actual facts; we should read the account from the Bible before going to see the movie.

There is an adorable song about unicorns that pertains to the flood. What is a unicorn? It is a cute little mythical horse-like animal which has a horn growing out of the top of its nose. In the song we learn that the unicorn was God's favorite animal, but when Noah called the animals into the ark, the unicorns ignored Noah, and just kept on playing and splashing in the water. Needless to say they didn't get on board, and that is why to this very day, you'll never see a unicorn. Cute song!

I like songs that tell stories, and I hear songs where I work, and hearing the vocalists repeat the same line over and over, and over, I ask myself, "Doesn't anyone know how to write lyrics anymore?" Some customers even comment on it, and one asked me once how I could stand to listen to that all day? I told her I only work four or five hours. She gave me an interesting look which indicated that that was too long.

Are there no longer songwriters like Rodgers and Hart? Cole Porter? Jerome Kerr? Jerry Herman? I remember songs when I was a teenager! Are you ready for these? "Singing The Blues," "The Little White Cloud That Cried," "How Much Is That Doggie In The Window?," "Standing On The Corner, Watching All The Girls Go By," "There's A Pawn Shop On The Corner In Pittsburgh Pennsylvania," "We'll Have These Moments To Remember," "I Could Have Danced All Night" from "My Fair Lady," and I could go on, but you probably don't want me to. These songs told stories; they were not just 'one liners.'

Will you remember the pop hit songs with titles and lyrics that you are listening to now?

I wonder if the individuals will remember the songs that I hear coming from their cars when they stop next to my car at a traffic intersection. First I feel the vibration from their cars, then the noise, and then the obscene language all of which penetrates my car and my senses.

I recall a movie star on a talk show; can't be sure, but it was either Michael Douglas or Martin Sheen, saying that when that happens to him, he turns up his Mozart. Apparently some movie stars are annoyed by this, too. Now I don't feel so bad.

The sound system in my car doesn't have that magnitude or capability, or I could turn up Yanni or Glen Miller's Big Band Selection, "Chattanooga Choo Choo" would really 'rock.' My all-time favorite of Glen Miller's arrangements is "In The Mood"; great song to dance to.

I am aware that there are many talented country western artists that have written songs that tell stories too, and some are beautiful ballads, but I am not a fan of Country Music.

I know that I could never write a musical piece, but perhaps I will put 'writing a screenplay' on my bucket list.

When We Walk 'It' Alone

Something I remember as a little girl: I was seven, maybe eight when I started to take piano lessons. My piano teacher lived on a neighboring farm which was to the south of our farm, and I needed to walk the length of a hay field to take lessons. To put the length of the field in proper perspective, I would compare it to almost the length of two football fields.

My mother or father would take me by car only in the event of rain, and of course during the winter. Otherwise, every Saturday afternoon I would take that very long walk through the hay field. It wasn't so scary until the hay grew, and then I was afraid of what I might step on. I would hear things in the hay - perhaps field mice. I always hoped there weren't any snakes.

Sometimes I would sing in hopes of scaring away anything that was underfoot. When it came time for 'haying,' my father would mow the hay, and I could see what was underfoot again.

One summer, something new appeared! Some huge new high power lines had been strung diagonally across the field. I remember that Saturday when I looked up and counted the wires; there were five. Five! Like five fingers on a hand. I imagined the mighty hand of God was watching over me, so why should I fear this long walk?

I am not sure what song I sang then, but this one would have been appropriate: "My God and I walk through the fields together; we walk and talk as good friends should and do."

I must say, though, I was very happy when my piano teacher and her husband moved off their farm, and built a new house near our church.

Through those 48 'life experiencing' years, I have many times encountered feelings of uncertainty and have been unsure of what was up ahead, but I could always envision those five high power lines, and what they represented to this little girl.

Now that I am attending my home church again I occasionally look to the east, and there those high power lines are still towering over the fields.

God's Grace is amazing, and the song is beautiful.

"Amazing Grace, how sweet the sound; that saved a wretch like me! I once was lost, but now am found; was blind, but now I see. Through many dangers, toils, and snares; I have already come; 'tis grace hath brought me safe thus far; and grace will lead me home."

Because songs reveal such beautiful messages, I want to share one more.

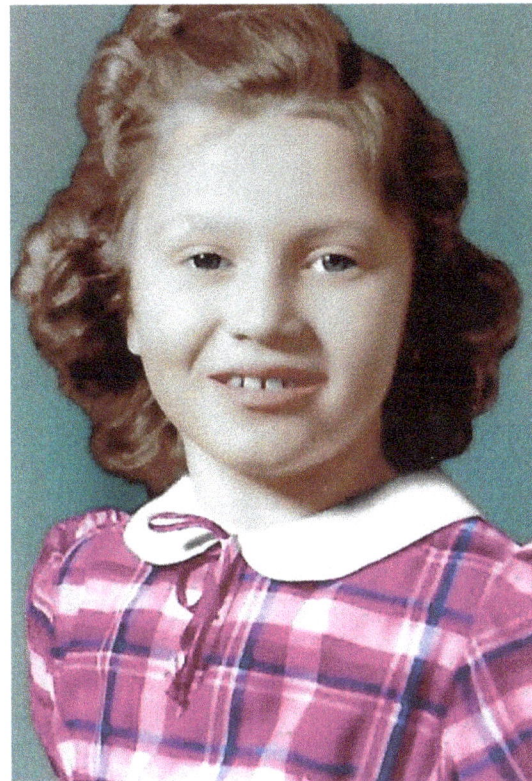

"When You Walk Through A Storm, keep your head up high, and don't be afraid of the dark; walk on walk on with hope in your heart, and you'll never walk alone!"

We read in James 4:8, "Draw near to God, and He will draw near to you."

Through Sun and Clouds, and Rain and Rainbows, stay close to the Lord, and the Lord will stay close to you!

All my Love and God's Blessings Forever!
Grandma Patricia

Patricia R. Frank has worn 'many hats' on her voyage of experiencing life. Her deep rooted faith, which many times had been gravely tested, has not only sustained her, but has persevered, and to some degree has inspired her to be commissioned with the words: "Here I Am Lord, I Will Go Lord, if You lead me. I will hold Your people in my heart." "While Grandma Is Sleeping" reaches out to those whose faith has been challenged, tested, and could virtually be on the brink of oblivion. Her prayer is that grandparents share with their grandchildren as she has shared with her grandchildren, now ages 17 to 28.

www.ingramcontent.com/pod-product-compliance
Lightning Source LLC
Chambersburg PA
CBHW040854100426
42813CB00015B/2799